W. H Metcalf

A Summer in Oldport Harbor

A Novel

W. H Metcalf

A Summer in Oldport Harbor
A Novel

ISBN/EAN: 9783744717199

Printed in Europe, USA, Canada, Australia, Japan

Cover: Foto ©Thomas Meinert / pixelio.de

More available books at **www.hansebooks.com**

A SUMMER

IN

OLDPORT HARBOR.

A NOVEL.

BY

W. H. METCALF.

PHILADELPHIA:
J. B. LIPPINCOTT COMPANY.
1887.

CONTENTS.

3

CHAPTER VI.

CHAPTER VII.

CHAPTER VIII.

CHAPTER IX.

CHAPTER X.

CHAPTER XI.

1*

A

SUMMER IN OLDPORT HARBOR.

CHAPTER I.

Jack in Trouble—Cup Island—The Home of the Hunters—Children as Judges of Character—Oldport and Vicinity—North Rock and Bogus Island—Extracts from Belle's Letter—The Sandy Cottage—Music on the Waters.

IT was Jack that was screaming at the top of his voice; but the doctor, although he heard him well enough, did not heed his cries, for it was a very common thing to hear Jack scream; in fact, since they were encamped upon the island, Jack was screaming or singing most of the time.

"Doc! Oh, Doc!" came again from above.

"Hello!" shouted the doctor, finally, in reply.

"Come up here, and help me with this boot, will you?" yelled Jack, in the clear, vigorous tones of a minaret crier of the far East.

The doctor hesitated a moment, for he was just in the act of rinsing out the coffee-pot when the idea occurred to him that perhaps his friend was

7

really in trouble; so, dropping the coffee-pot, he bounded hastily up the narrow stairway, five steps at a time.

The little house contained but two rooms, one below, upon the ground-floor, and one above, which they were using for a sleeping apartment. The stairway was at the rear, and outside of the house proper, but was boxed in with boards so that one could pass from one room to the other under cover.

When Tom, or the doctor, arrived in the upper chamber, he found Jack flat upon his back, his face redder than a Berkshire sunset, his chest heaving with over-exertion, puffing and squirming as though in mortal agony, and with great beads of perspiration rolling down his brow.

"What is the matter, old boy?" said Tom.

Jack ceased wriggling for a moment, while with a look pathetic enough to have melted the heart of an angry mother-in-law, he said, in a subdued tone,—

"Doc, for heaven's sake release my foot from that chair; it is caught, and I have been struggling to get it out for ten or fifteen minutes."

Telling him to lie still, and drawing closer, Tom took in the whole situation at a glance. Jack, having been unable to pull off his wet boots, and not possessing a boot-jack, had improvised one out of an old hair-cloth rocking-chair, which was

a part of their common stock of furniture. By
lying upon his back on the floor, and placing his
foot between the rocker and the bottom of the
seat, toe up, he had succeeded in drawing off one
of the refractory boots; but when he endeavored
to do likewise with the other, the integrity of the
chair-bottom gave way, wedging his toe in between the coils of a stiff spiral spring, and jam-
ming his heel still tighter upon the rocker. In
this predicament Tom found him. By drawing up
the spring a little, and carefully turning the captive foot, it was at length released, Tom meantime
reading the prostrate giant a lecture upon the im-
propriety of placing one's feet unwarily in strange
places.

Jack was a good-natured soul. He had been
reared in the same town with Tom. As boys together they had cemented a friendship which had
grown with the passing years. They had fostered a
mutual regard which had its beginnings in youthful
indiscretions. The same bond of sympathy which
as orchard depredators had tied their friendships
had, by that curious dispensation which so often
transforms the bad boy into the noble man, developed into an affectionate regard and admiration
for true manly qualities. Jack, as he approached
maturity, went abroad to study art in Florence,
and about the same time Tom attended an American college nearer home. It so happened that

they did not again meet for years, and when they
did, it was in New York city, at the table of a
mutual friend. Jack had settled in the city as an
artist, and Tom as an aspiring young physician
with a growing practice. Their first meeting or
reunion was the signal for the renewal of their
old friendship, and they were afterward much together; in fact, they hired common apartments,
and became as comfortable and happy as two
moderately successful young bachelors could be.
A little over two years they had led this life,
working diligently at their respective professions
and allowing themselves a very limited supply of
recreation. One day, toward the middle of July,
Jack proposed that they should take a vacation,
throw away all care, and unrestrainedly woo the
muses. This proposition suited Tom exactly, the
more so since there was just at that time a young
fellow-classmate, who had been assisting him in
hospital duties, who could take charge of his practice during his absence.

Tom and Jack both needed recreation, for they
began to feel the strain of continued application.
It was therefore with light hearts that they laid
out their plans for an eight-weeks' vacation.
Tom's family owned a small island, containing
perhaps twenty-five acres, and situated near the
Connecticut shore in Long Island Sound. His
father, before he died, had been in the habit of

visiting this island in the fall of each year with a
party of·friends, to fish and shoot ducks.   There
he had built or "thrown together" a small frame
shanty or cottage of two rooms, which, roughly
furnished, served for shelter and made the sports-
men tolerably comfortable.   Here it was, upon
Cup Island, that Tom and his friend Jack decided
to enjoy their eight weeks of leisure.

Cup Island was once probably a bare rock; but
time, aided by the perpetually restless winds and
tides, had covered its surface with several feet of
alluvial soil, out of which trees and bushes had
sprung up, making it withal a place picturesque
and attractive.

At flood-tide Cup Island seemed to consist of
three distinct islands; but when the tide was low,
it was possible to walk from one end to the other
without seriously wetting the soles of the feet.   It
lay about a third of a mile from the Connecticut
shore; and lying near it, at perhaps a distance of
three hundred yards, was another and smaller
island, owned by a wealthy Connecticut gentleman, who resided in one of the interior towns of
the State.   Smoke Island, as it was called by the
natives thereabouts, was much smaller than the
one upon which Tom and Jack were to sojourn,—
perhaps one-half the size.   Major Van Twist, the
owner, with his wife and only daughter, Alice,
occasionally spent a summer there, where he had

erected a very comfortable and commodious cottage, with every convenience which could be arranged in such a place.

Every nook and corner of these islands became familiar to Tom in his boyhood, when he had accompanied his father on his duck-shooting excursions. At these times he had been instructed in the management of a boat, the use of a gun and fishing-tackle, and the by no means non-essential, though rudimentary, knowledge of the culinary art.

There were times during the early morning hours when it was too cold for him to lie in wait for ducks with the others. On these occasions he would assist the mulatto cook, from whom he learned many secrets in cookery, and on the return of the hungry hunters his skill was often praised, and he was pronounced a gastronomical prodigy.

How jolly they seemed of an evening, as they gathered around the steaming punch-bowl to relate the experiences of the day just past. Some smoking their long-stemmed pipes, the vigorous wood fire sending forth its myriads of quick, bright sparks, while the long-tongued flames lapped the chimney back so smoothly, till with a roar they would instantly vanish up the dark flue above. The recollection of those happy times, of those ruddy, good-natured faces, made more rosy by the

red glow of the brisk, warm fire; of the exciting
stories which often brought such hearty laughter
or applause; of those happy in-door nights upon
Cup Island, brought back to Tom the same sense
of confiding dependence, the same feeling of perfect security and trustfulness which had so mas-
tered his heart as a boy. Well did he remember
how fiercely the elements would rage outside of
that little cottage on those autumn nights. Sometimes the little house actually rocked under the
strain, and then, who could laugh louder or longer
than these half-dozen strong men, who were
lounging in restful attitudes about the ample fireplace?

> " The housemates sit
> Around the radiant fireplace enclosed
> In a tumultuous privacy of storm."

Then there were nights when Tom, lying in the
little upper chamber of the cottage and listening
to the distant roar of the elements and the nearer
sonorous breathing of his father's friends, would
speculate upon his own chances of ever reaching
such a glorious manhood as theirs. How well he
loved them all, this whole-hearted boy.

Could the mature half of humanity possess both
the capacity to feel and the ability to understand
the youthful heart, how easy of solution would be
the problem of child-management. How different,
and how much more effective, would be the method

2

of rearing, instructing, and guiding children. There is, no doubt, some truth in the statement that children are under the continual guidance and constant care of heavenly angels. Certainly their bright looks, happy moods, their beauty, and their innocent and uncontrollable way of wearing love on the surface, all of these winning traits seem to bear out the thought. Perhaps they *are* under the direct guardianship of God's companions, else why should they in their tender years evince such wonderful capacity in the judgment and discrimination of character?—a trait they often sadly lose later in life. Are not their evil moods but harbingers of advancing maturity, when the physical supplants the spiritual, or the human crowds back the angelic? Could we but think so, perhaps second childhood, as we often see it in extreme old age, would lose much of its unsightliness.

It is easy to guarantee the moral worth of a stranger when we notice that he is generally loved by little children. On the other hand, if the little ones fear or seem to instinctively avoid a person, how easy and natural it is to suspect that "there is a screw loose somewhere." If a person is genuine in his fondness for children, putting himself out, perhaps, to please them, not in a studied way, but spontaneously, naturally, how pleasing it is to us as fathers, mothers, sisters, brothers, or relatives to single him out from among men as one to be trusted and safely loved. On the other hand, it would be difficult to find in history a man who has won the hearts of the people and disliked little children. A child is the symbol of innocence; therefore, to love a child is to love innocence.

Some such thoughts as these coursed through the doctor's mind as he selected Cup Island for their summer resort. Their preparations for departure began immediately. A few days to arrange the affairs of office and studio previous to so prolonged an absence, a day or two to collect traps and luggage essential to such a pleasure trip, and they were ready to depart.

It was on the early morning train from New York, on the "Shore Line Railroad," that they started for Oldport, on the 19th of July, and a few hours brought them safely to their destination. Oldport, which was the nearest village to Cup Island, certainly did not belie its name, either in the appearance of its ancient-looking streets and houses or the peculiar characteristics of its inhabitants. The railroad did not profane the immediate precincts of the place, the station being at least two miles from the centre of the village. Indeed, one would hardly know where the centre of the place was were it not generally understood that the grocery and post-office served as a sort of landmark for that important locality. The doctor and his friend Jack took more than an ordinary interest in the surroundings; and this was natural, since they had come to live for the greater part of the summer so near to the quaint old town.

Sending their luggage ahead, therefore, in the grocery wagon, which, by the way, also carried the mail and was a thing to be relied upon at every train, they strolled along the country road until they reached the village proper, taking careful and accurate mental notes of all they saw and heard.

Jack, as became an artist, was in ecstasies over the many picturesque views which caught his eye, pausing often to admire and comment upon a rustic bridge or gateway, or a few sleek and robust cattle browsing upon a sunlit stretch of bright green meadow or reclining lazily upon the side of a grass-covered hillock. Now a high-gabled farmhouse of antique proportions, nestling under the protecting shade of a brace of buttonwood-trees, with its usual accompaniments of red barn and old-fashioned well, would bring him to a pause spellbound with admiration. Occasionally the familiar farm dog, an animal of large proportions and shaggy coat, would rouse itself from slumber and walk lazily toward them with a look in its eye of mistrust until it comprehended their friendly greetings.

Tom was particularly amused by the people.

They passed a couple of farm lads with their red, freckled faces almost hidden under the broadest of straw hats, whose rims rose and fell, as the lads walked, ludicrously like the ears of the mule which they were leading. Soon after this they passed a farm-house and noticed in the door-yard a buxom, large-limbed maiden suspending the week's washing upon a line which she had stretched from one apple-tree to another. As she worked she sang to herself a well-worn distich from "Pinafore" about "A merry, merry maiden and a tar," when suddenly, becoming aware of the proximity of our young friends, she ceased her melody and made a conspicuous effort to creep in out of herself, the gracefulness of which must be seen in country maidens to be thoroughly appreciated.

Thus collecting food for future discourse and entertainment, they finally came to the village post-office. It was the typical country post-office, useless to describe because so familiar. A grocery in the rear, where from the same shelf calico came to the light of day with dried herrings; where butter, cheese, beer, nails, candy, hosiery, cigars, and cat, all reposed upon a common counter. A heterogeneous display of the necessities of life, all within ready reach of the slow-moving proprietor, upon whose shrewd Yankee visage one could see stamped a corresponding type of incongruity. There seemed nothing wanting to supply the needs of micro-

cosmic man in this haven of rusticity save per-
chance a postmaster. But, behold! the same
wizard, Samuel Sandy by name, who, after dealing
out sugar and oil in quantities to suit your convenience, will take nine slowly-measured steps to
the front of this establishment, where he will disappear into a little cubby-hole of a place on the
right and transform himself into a model country
postmaster, possessing the requisite modicum of
" inquisitive curiosity."

Time was at a discount in Oldport. Fifteen
minutes to buy a two-cent stamp was *in rerum
natura* a reasonable wait. Three-quarters of an
hour to sort a mail of seven postal cards and a
half-dozen letters was to the patient native a *nolens
volens*. Had he not the blessed privilege of con-
soling himself with the charitable thought that
the worthy postmaster was not overtaxing himself,
but was industriously cramming his ample brains
with postal-card lore? Why should he shorten
his precious life by unnecessary and uncalled-for
speed? It has been rumored that the people of
Oldport never formally die, that their demise is
a process so gradual and continuous, or, as the
French would say, *à propos de rien*, as to be hardly
perceptible,—a method of slow withering until a
period of desiccation is reached, in connection
with which it taxes mortal scrutiny to discover
one in the act of departure. Certain it is, our

young friends did not see a soul there who had anything like a lucid recollection of a funeral.

The store was not far from the beach where they were to embark, so, after the necessary negotiations for the use of boats during their stay at Cup Island, in which the *de facto* heterogenarian took an active interest (for besides his multifarious mercantile proclivities, Sam Sandy owned and let out boats), they jumped into the store-wagon, and were driven to the shore. From the pier upon the beach both islands were in sight, Smoke Island being partially hidden behind her sister. The day was beautiful, the water placid, with enough breeze to freshen the air, which, with the bright sunlight reflecting the white sails of a score of craft in the distance, added picturesqueness to the scene and vigor to our city friends who witnessed it.

Mr. Sandy had locked up the store and post-office, "just for safety, ye know," as he remarked, and had accompanied them to the beach, where, from an assortment of two, one of which leaked outrageously, they selected a row-boat. He promised to bring them a sailboat on the following day at noon, a "reel clipper," as he designated her. He said, "I've hauled her up fur a few days ter give 'er a coat of paint."

A short row of perhaps ten minutes brought them with their belongings to Cup Island, where they were soon snugly installed in their new home.

It was now about ten o'clock in the forenoon; so after unpacking some of their things, they sallied forth upon the island to explore a little before dinner. Tom noticed few changes of great importance. Here and there some one had built a bench or rustic chair, and quite a substantial landing-place or pier had been put up for the landing of people from boats.

The tide was high, but they found a rough bridge of timber thrown across the water, connecting North Rock, as it was called, with the centre or main part of the island. This little north island consisted of a huge boulder-like rock, sloping upward perhaps thirty feet from the water in a gradual ascent. On the sea side this rise was more abrupt, but there were shelving ridges, along which one could safely walk, and which afforded inviting seats where it was possible to fish or meditatively watch the sea.

When the tide was low this rock was a part of the main island, and one could easily walk there over the moist rocks; but now the water was rushing swiftly under the little bridge and against the sides of the rocks, as if anxious not to be left behind in the tide of ocean affairs.

At the south end of Cup Island they found a little cove, with a shelving beach. At flood-tide this little cove or bay extended quite across the island, separating the south end also into a distinct island, which they named Bogus Island. It was much larger and more inviting than North Rock, having upon it a number of small trees which struggled for existence, and a neat little summer-house. From this summer-house was a delightful view of the sound, a distant view of the Connecticut coast, and a more extended one of Long Island. They shoved themselves across the narrow channel to Bogus Island in the boat, sat for a few moments in the summer-house, and then returning to the cottage, began to make preparations for dinner.

Having eaten little since their early meal in the city, they both possessed good appetites, which condition served as a stimulus to activity in the production of their repast, more than to elaborate care in the details of its preparation.

Jack, true to his Bohemian instincts, made the coffee with artistic precision, while Tom spread indiscriminately upon the table a hearty supply of the substantials and delicacies with which their box of provisions was stored. From these things, so roughly served, they proceeded to extract that inexpressible satisfaction known only to those who have been placed in similar happy circumstances.

" Well," said Jack, as he was finishing, and with a sigh of contentment producing an ample meerschaum pipe, in which he proceeded to pack the bright golden flakes of Virginia smoking tobacco, "is not this about the perfection of comfort and independence?"

"Jack," replied Tom, following his friend's example and producing a cigar, "as I advance into the fulness of manhood, into the roundness of maturity, I realize more and more fully the joys of living and companionship."

"And eating," Jack replied; "for where would be fulness and the roundness without? Yea, even the manhood or maturity?"

"I think you are right," Tom replied, laughing; and then lapsing unconsciously into a philosophical mood born of repletion, "Yet, how strange seems the fact that on this mundane sphere there exist beings who hold eating and drinking to be vulgar, when the very *vis vitæ* of existence is helplessly dependent upon this function."

"Yes," said Jack, lazily, behind a cloud of smoke, but with a facetious twinkle in his handsome blue eyes, "Arnold says, you know, in his 'Light of Asia,' 'How lizard fed on ant, and snake on him, and kite on both; and how the fish-hawk robbed the fish-tiger of that which it had seized; the shrike chasing the bulbul, which did chase the jewelled butterflies; till everywhere each slew a slayer, and in turn was slain, life living upon death.' Nature is indeed but a huge mother-gourmand, a sort of cannabalistic gormandizer, whose myriad children industriously devour each other as from a sense of duty. Scientists have dubbed this voracious faculty 'the conservation of forces and matter,' and some materialists, with whom I am not at all inclined to differ, base their plausible theory of 'the survival of the fittest' upon this very law."

Jack's materialism had for some time been a source of anxiety to the doctor; and had he followed his first impulse he would have given him a sharp reply to this last sally; but his better instincts prevailed, and decided him to await a more favorable opportunity, so he simply said good-humoredly, " By the way, Jack, who is to wash these dishes ? They certainly have a very material look about them."

" As a dish-washer I have been a success," replied Jack.

" Then I will be your successor," said Tom ; " and these horny hands of labor shall make the dishes shine like the bald pates of your paternal ancestry."

" And while you do it," Jack said, with a hearty laugh, " I, whom the Fates have decreed should be a maid-of-all-work, since all work seems made for me, will hie me to the guest-chamber above, and prepare our downy couch for its restless occupants."

" All right," said the doctor. " By the way, you

will find mattresses in the old chest in the corner, and also blankets enough to make Morpheus grin with lazy joy. Here is the key."

The following few hours were devoted to fixing up their quarters, and they soon considered themselves comfortably settled, barring, of course, the little inconveniences which one naturally expects and even welcomes on such occasions.

At about three in the afternoon they took the boat and rowed over to Oldport to see if there might be some mail for them at the post-office.

Tom found a few lines from his assistant, asking advice upon some matters concerning his practice, and a letter postmarked " W——, Mass.," directed in his sister Belle's handwriting to Dr. Thomas Tillottson, Oldport, Connecticut. This he opened speedily, fearing that his mother, who had been quite ill of late, might be worse.

Judge of his surprise when he reached a part of the letter which read as follows :

"And now, dear Tom, rejoice in what I have to tell you next. Dr. Perry says that mamma *must* have sea air, that an immediate change is imperative, and that she should stay by the salt water until the hottest of the weather is past. Now, dear old Tom, what *shall* we do, and where *can* we go, unless to Oldport, where we can be with you? The worst of it is, Nettie Knowles (my old room-mate at school, you remember) has just arrived here to make me a long visit. I have told her the circumstances, and she is willing and even anxious to go to Oldport with us. Mamma says, if we hear favorably from you, that we can all go together, and she will take Bid along to cook for us. Now, Tom, dear, be real good, and say that Nettie and I can come to the cottage and camp out with you and Mr. Stratton. Oh, it would be delightful. Mamma and Aunt Deborah can board in Oldport, and we can see them every day. Oh, Tom, if you only will say yes, I will bless you all the mortal days of my existence and hug you to death. Just think of it. Nettie and I can do lots and lots of things for you and your friend, and we will catch fish for dinner: and now, Tom, dear, you will not say no, will you, but hunt up a nice boarding-place near the water for mamma and send for us right away. Bid can sleep most anywhere. Nettie says she remembers you *perfectly*, although she only saw you two or three minutes, and I know you will like her, for she is just the dearest angel living. Answer at once, and say *come*.

" Your loving, yearning sister,

" Boots."

Boots was rather a strange pet name for a brother to give his young lady sister ; but, though not particularly elegant, it was not altogether inappropriate, as its origin will show.

Many years before, when Belle was a little curly-haired child of three or four summers, she had wandered down-stairs in a spirit of mischievousness, long after the family had supposed her sound asleep, arrayed in her night-dress and a pair of Tom's boots. Her appearance thus unexpectedly at all hours of the evening was not a very uncommon occurrence; and, although she knew it was contrary to the domestic laws of the establishment, she always escaped punishment by some comical act connected with her visit below-stairs. As she hobbled on this occasion into the brilliantly-lighted parlor where the family and a few invited guests were assembled, she succeeded in creating a sensation. She was soon smothered in the loving arms of one of the lady guests, from which position she was rescued by Tom, who called her his little Boots as he carried her back to bed. From that time the name clung to her, at least whenever Tom addressed her, and thus it was that the beautiful Belle Tillottson was called by her brother, Boots.

Tom was very much surprised at the letter. His first inclination was to send them word that it would be impossible in such a small place to accommodate so many, but reflection caused him to change his mind. He was alarmed about the reported illness of his mother and desirous to have her near him, where, if necessary, he could administer his professional skill. So, after showing or reading the letter to Jack, they both agreed that it would be only fair to see if a suitable boarding-place could be obtained for Mrs. Tillottson. They therefore interviewed Mr. Sandy at once, asking him if he knew of a desirable place.

"Waal," said he to the doctor, slowly rubbing his red chin with the back of his redder hand, "if yer mammy ain't over pertickler, an' could git 'long 'th ordinery kind o' livin', I ruther incline to think my ole woman wouldn't go agin keepin' of her fur a few weeks. We live snug by the water yonder, 'an so we git a coolish breeze the better part of the hot weather. Ef yer like, we'll trot down an' tech the ole lady 'bout it."

Tom agreed; so they walked over to the Sandy residence, which was a comfortable frame cottage, painted a pale peacock-green, with reddish colored blinds. Mrs. Sandy was drawing water from the family well in front of the cottage. Tom stated the case to her briefly, and after a quick glance at the smiling face of her good husband, she said she thought she could accommodate the two ladies,' and led them to a comfortable room at a corner of the house, which overlooked the water on one side and commanded an extensive view of the street on the other.

After the necessary arrangements about terms, etc., Tom asked for writing materials, and imme-

diately indited a letter to his sister Belle, informing her that they could all come on at once. This
the postmaster waited for. As they were passing
out of the house they were met by a huge dog
with anything but a friendly look in his eyes.

"Don't be skeered on him," said Mr. Sandy.
"Here Sikey, lie down, sir." The dog sulked into
the house. "That is the meanest dorg out," he
continued. "He was fetched to me by an ole
sailor, a mate o' mine, from across the water. He
is a cross atween a Sain' Bernard an' a blood-
hound; an' when he fust come, he'd chase the
cattle almost to death an' destruction; but I cured
him, I did, didn't I, wife?" Mrs. Sandy nodded
approvingly.

"How did you cure him, Mr. Sandy?" asked
Jack.

"Waal, fust I began to lick him whenever he
cut up them capers; but the critter didn't seem to
notice what I were lickin' him fur; so one day I
made up my mind I'd learn the cuss to obey. I
fetched him inter the barn, shet all the doors an'
threw a chunk o' meat on the floor, and told 'im
not to tetch it. Waal, he did tetch it, an' gobbled
it down at one gulp. Then I licked him for tetch-
in' it until he yelled. Then I flung another chunk
o' meat, an' telled him not to tetch that; but he
gobbled that right down the same as t'other, and
so I licked 'im agin. Waal, I kep droppin' chunk

arter chunk o' meat, an' he kep a gobblin' 'em right along, and I kep a lickin' on him like blazes, until, finally, I could stick a chunk right under the critter's nose an' he never offered to tetch it, or even smell of it. That's the way I cured that dorg, gentlemen. You can try it on any dorg you ever see, an' it'll allus work like a charm."

"Didn't it take a large quantity of meat?" asked Jack.

"Waal, yes," said Sandy, "it did; but it's only fur once, an' it's worth it."

After making arrangements with Mr. Sandy to bring them provisions every morning, including milk and bread, they returned to the boat.

"Here's a go!" shouted Jack, as they rowed back over the water. "What shall we do?"

"We must do the best we can," said Tom. "The girls and Bid must occupy the upper room, and we can sleep down-stairs on the floor, or hang ourselves upon nails in the chimney-corner."

"I will build a couple of bunks in a corner of the lower room," said Jack. "I noticed some loose boards under the house this morning, which will serve nicely for that purpose."

"No more dish-washing," said Tom, with a sigh of relief.

"And no more bed-making," said Jack, "nor care about how our grub must be cooked. I tell you, old fellow, it is a grand scheme, having them here. We will live like fighting-cocks and grow fat."

It was a few hours after this that Jack, coming in from one of his tramps in search of views for future work, went up-stairs to pull off his wet boots.

After supper they strolled out for a walk, Jack taking his banjo. They crossed the cove to Bogus Island in the boat, sat in the summer-house, and enjoyed the charming view to the east, south, and west of them. The evening was perfect. The surface of the water reflected in a thousand golden ripples the soft rays of the slowly-setting sun, which was now a huge ball of lurid fire in the glowing western sky.

Jack was in ecstasies; Tom inclined to revery. Thus they sat, occasionally conversing until long after the sun had disappeared behind the distant western hills. What a delightful contrast was this to their constrained life in the hot metropolis. Here that elixir of life, pure cool air, gave them strength and vigor, while the knowledge of the contrast to what they had endured in the city only made it more enjoyable.

Here, instead of the weary, limited view of bricks and mortar, was an unconfined expanse of water; in one direction hills and woods, in another an un-obstructed view of a sublime sunset to gaze upon.

When darkness in long sweeping shadows began

to gather around them Jack laid aside his pipe, and
in his clear tenor voice began to sing, accompanying himself upon the banjo. Tom joined in with
his rich bass voice.

It was their common practice at home to sing;
but never before had music seemed so gratifying as
here upon the quiet waters of Oldport Harbor.
Both being excellent singers, and Jack a master at
accompaniment, the melody which they produced
was well calculated to bring out the sleeping fairies
of the island and woo the water-nymphs to its
moss-bound shores. The sweet music wafted its
way over the peaceful harbor to the near-lying
coast, there mingling harmoniously with the gentle
beating of the incoming waves, while along the
country lanes and by-ways by the beach wooing
couples ceased their love-exchanges to imbibe the
precious melody, and the weary rustic on his way
to the well for his evening draught paused spellbound till the music ceased.

Who has not experienced the great charm of
music upon the waters at night? At such times
it seems as though the conditions by which music
may flow into the willing soul are all amply fulfilled. Our friends in the summer-house sang and
chatted until the chilly sea-air warned them to re-
tire to the cottage to spend their first night in the
country.

Ah, that first night! How the very thought of

it brings to the weary city-worn soul a sense of vigorous refreshment. No gasping at the wide-open casement for a breath of fresh air. No tossing upon hot linen in vain effort to secure a comfortable position. No lying with eyes wide open into the small hours of morning when the rumbling of early milk- and market-wagons attests to the nearness of daylight. None of these curses, but sleep, sweet, restful, uninterrupted sleep.

CHAPTER II.

Belle and her Friend—The Doctor's Letter to Boots—Mrs. Till-ottson—A short History of Miss Knowles—Boarding-school Friendship—Roger Dexter—Morning at Cup Island—Jack as he appeared to the Natives.

Two handsome girls were sitting in a low basket phaeton at the door of an unimposing-looking post-office in the town of W——, Massachusetts. They were awaiting the regular distribution of the morning mail. One, around whose white shapely arm the reins are twisted carelessly, whose broad-brimmed sun-hat failed to conceal the golden-hued· curls which had escaped bondage and were clustered around two deep-blue laughing eyes, whose rounded cheeks and graceful neck and matchless,

healthful complexion, and whose pouting, restless
lips bespoke a life of fun, frolic, and incessant
activity; this young lady, with her broad shoulders
and shapely figure, a Venus in modern trapery,
was Isabel Tillottson, Tom's sister.

By her side, a trifle shorter in stature, but not
less striking in face or figure, sat her friend, Nettie
Knowles. People said on seeing them together,—
"What a beautiful contrast. Behold evening
and morning."

Miss Knowles had brown eyes, with hair as
black as night itself. Her complexion was dark,
but full of bloom. No sluggish or lymphatic blood
coursed through her veins; yet, while one viewed
her, expecting momentarily vivacity and excitement, there was an air of pure contentment and
self-possession, a look of sweet repose, about her
which told the story of a true life well spent, and
a future of noble exertions. A glance at these
two specimens of fascinating girlhood as they sat
innocently chatting in the neat little phaeton, would
have sufficed to transform the most hardened foreign skeptic into a willing panegyrist upon the
beauty of these, America's maidens.

The short, compact, dignified little roan pony,
to whom Miss Belle occasionally addressed a
caressing word, though apparently troubled by
the inevitable summer flies, acted and looked full
appreciation of the importance and responsibility

c

which devolved upon him as the bearer of such precious freight. He stamped his feet, switched his apology for a caudal appendage, vigorously shook the solid muscles of his shoulders, occasionally turning his head backward for a moment, and with soulful eyes looking gratitude at Nettie, who industriously brushed off the venomous flies with the end of the whip. How well he knew that the weapon was never put to a more serious use. Tobey was a good pony, and well deserved the care and affection which were lavished upon him by his human acquaintances.

A slight commotion among the people gathered about the post-office indicated that the distribution of the mail had begun. Miss Tillottson jumped lightly out of the vehicle, and, after disappearing for a few moments, returned with the family mail.

"See, Nettie," cried she joyfully, stepping at the same time briskly into the phaeton, "a letter from Tom. I knew he would answer promptly, and I feel that it contains good news for us. Keep the reins. Now, drive Tobey slowly and I will read the letter." This without further ceremony she proceeded to do.

Her look of eager curiosity soon changed, and a pleased smile illuminated her beautiful face as she read, and before she had reached the end, and as she finished, her whole countenance was wreathed

in smiles.   She burst into a hearty laugh, and said
to her friend Nettie,—

"I will read what the dear boy says.   He is too
good for anything, but you must not tell that I
betrayed confidence, will you?"

"Honor bright," said Nettie, mysteriously, and
Belle then read as follows:

"DEAR BOOTS,—To say that the contents of
your letter surprised me would be drawing it too
mildly.   I was annihilated, discombobolated, and
for a while helplessly paralyzed.   Why, Jack and
I were hardly settled in our rough (very rough)
quarters when along comes your bombshell of a
letter, upsetting all of our arrangements and over-
throwing all of our plans.   We fly from petticoat-
infested Gotham, seeking the seclusion sacred of a
deserted isle, when before we have slept upon our
relieved condition in pops your epistle upon us,
and with visions of petticoats innumerable.   There,
now, don't cry.   Of course you may come, Boots;
you always did do just as you wanted, and always
will, I suppose, as long as you have such a weak-
headed, easily-ridden brother.   Jack does not seem
to feel bad about your prospective raid, so I guess I
won't care;   besides, I have not entirely forgotten
the bright vision of a round, pretty face, with deep
inquiring hazel eyes peering out of its upper story,
which greeted me when I visited your school.   I

have carried *them* eyes about with me ever since. Yes, I have, in my vest-pocket,—the upper left. Now, don't go and tell Miss Knowles all this, Boots, for you know I only saw her for a moment. I wonder if she remembers me? Seriously, though, Boots, do you think you girls can stand it at the cottage? You have been here, you know, and can best judge whether your friend will be able to endure the inconveniences.

"I have found a place for mother and Aunt Deb near the beach in Oldport. Bid can be accommodated at the cottage, I guess. Mother's room is at the house of a man of astounding accomplishments, one Sandy by name and appearance. Samuel Sandy has sandy hair and complexion. The Sandy cottage is close upon a sandy beach, and is, withal, about as snug and comfortable a place as mother could desire or expect in such an antiquated, out-of-the-way neighborhood.

"I write in haste to catch the down mail. You will receive this in the morning. Come on the noon train next Wednesday, the day after to-morrow, and please bring extra bedding along for two or three. Jack says he will rig up some Oriental bunks in the scullery *à la* Chinese; but we don't agree to do the washing. Bring a bottle of whiskey and some court-plaster; we may need both.

"Ever your loving

"THOMAS CAT."

" Now, didn't I tell you the dear boy couldn't refuse me ?" said Belle, gleefully. " He is just too good for anything. Think of it, Nettie, what an awful bore it will be to those men,—having two girls roughing it out on that island !"

" Perhaps we had better give it up after all ?" said Nettie, whose heart failed her when she thought of being a trouble to anybody.

" No, indeed; we cannot give up going now," replied Belle, " for there is mamma, you know, who must have a change. The doctor has ordered sea-air; so now we must make the best of the little time we have before to-morrow, in order to get everything ready." Then, still seeing a look of doubt on Nettie's countenance, she continued,—

" We can be of the greatest use to Tom and Mr. Stratton, you know, dear. We will see that the house is kept tidy, and that the cooking is good, and before we have been on the island twenty-four hours they will be glad enough that we came."

" It is rather strange that he should have re-membered me so long," Nettie said, half to her-self.

" Not at all strange, you dear little goose," said Belle, accompanying her remark with a kiss. " He did nothing but talk of you for a whole week after we reached home."

" But he only saw me for a moment or two,

4

and then there were several other girls in the room."

"Not like my sweet old Net," said Belle, lovingly. "Isn't it good of Jack—I mean Mr. Stratton—to make those Oriental booths in the lower room of the cottage?"

"Bunks, you mean," said Nettie, laughing.

"Well, bunks," said Belle, "whatever they are. But I forgot, Nettie, that you had never seen the place. I hope you will not be disappointed. It is horribly inconvenient; but it is lovely there on the island, and the views are so exquisite that one soon forgets everything unpleasant."

"I am certain, Belle, that if you are pleased and happy there, I shall be," said Nettie.

Thus chatting, as they rode along, occasionally stopping at some dry-goods establishment or grocery to purchase some of the things which they needed for their journey, and which they had carefully written down upon a piece of paper, they finally reached home, where they imparted the good news to Mrs. Tillottson.

Belle's mother was a lady of striking appearance. In figure tall and majestic, with a face of uncommon sweetness and serenity, she was a lady who always commanded respect from those with whom she came in contact. Her voice was one of her chief charms. She never vaporized nor adopted high accents; but whenever she spoke there was to the listener a soothing effect like that caused by the summer wind breathing softly through grateful foliage. Her manner was always easy and unconstrained; and this gracious gift was particularly noticeable on those occasions when a slight stiffness or formality might be expected and perfectly excusable. In this she differed materially from the great majority of ladies of her own age, who, when taken unawares or in emergencies, lose in manner and presence of mind. But perhaps the most noticeable virtue of this sweet woman was her great love for the society of young people.

Her house was always open to them, and they in their turn were glad to be in her company. A subtle something in her manner of receiving their overtures seemed to win their youthful hearts at once, and with their hearts their full and unrestrained confidence. If secrets were kept from others, they were never withheld from Aunt Mary, as she was called by all of her young acquaintances. She in her turn was always faithful, and true to her trust, although a sort of repository for all sorts of information. Youthful lovers always found sympathy with Aunt Mary. Was there a new baby in town, Aunt Mary knew of it first, and, moreover, would be the first to see that its mother was comfortable. Was there sickness or suffering, she was the ever-present ministering angel. It is easy to understand, therefore, why Aunt Mary was very much beloved by the good people of W——.

With the occasional exception of a short trip to New York or Boston, she had been away from W—— very little since her husband's death, ten years previous; therefore, when her physician advised and urged her to go to the sea-shore for a few weeks, she naturally felt reluctant about leaving her home. Her daughter, Belle, however, with her happy thoughtfulness, suggested going to Oldport, and the prospect of joining her son Tom had entirely reconciled her to the idea of leaving. She consequently awaited his reply with almost as much anxiety and interest as the two young ladies.

Judge of her pleasure, then, when they came joyfully bustling into her presence with Tom's welcome letter.

"Now, girls," said she, after reading it attentively, "is the time for action. There is much to be accomplished before to-morrow morning. I will trust you to collect the things we shall necessarily need during our absence, while I see that the household affairs are left in proper condition, for you know Aunt Deborah is going with us."

It is needless to describe the busy bustle of preparation into which they now threw themselves. Nettie was by no means a useless guest, neither did she require the contagion of activity as an incentive to action. With her, mind and body were completely subservient to will, and her will was always good.

Here, perhaps, it may be best to give the reader something of her previous history.

Nettie Knowles was an orphan. About fifteen years previous, her father, then a missionary of considerable reputation, and settled at Honolulu, in the Hawaiian Islands, died, leaving an invalid widow, and Nettie, his daughter, then little more than two years of age. Mrs. Knowles, his widow, unable to endure the first fierce agonies of grief at her bereavement, became more feeble,—could not even seem to rally for her child's sake, to meet again the struggles of the world. She lingered between life and death a few short weeks, and finally followed her husband, leaving her little girl alone, and in a foreign land. The American consul, a man of large heart and noble impulses, took little Nettie into his own family, writing, as he had promised her mother he would, to the child's nearest relative in the United States. Adam Dexter, to whom the letter was addressed, was a widower, and the brother of Mrs. Knowles. He lived in G——, one of the flourishing towns in Central New York, where, by prudence, energy, and fate, he had amassed a considerable fortune as a manufacturer. He had one son, Roger, then a youth

of perhaps ten years. To this uncle of Nettie's
came the sad intelligence of the death of Mr. and
Mrs. Knowles, and the destitute condition of their
child. He was not a man to hesitate when duty
demanded his services; therefore, he immediately
started for Honolulu, and in less than three months
little Nettie was comfortably settled at her uncle's
as his adopted daughter.

She was too young to miss her parents long.
Time, that obliterator of human sorrow, soon
taught her to regard Mr. Dexter as a father, and
she loved him with all the affection of a daughter.

Shortly after her fourteenth anniversary Mr.
Dexter sent her to a fashionable boarding-school
in Massachusetts, where she met and became
strongly attached to Belle Tillottson, her room-
mate and fellow-student. Thus, thrown so closely
together, and both possessing affectionate, clinging
natures, they formed a friendship, which, unlike
the ordinary school-girl attachments, was destined
to last as long as life itself.

The year previous to the time when we now see
them at W——, they had graduated from school
and parted, each going to her own home; but
their mutual love was too strong to allow a long
separation, and Belle had spent the greater part of
the winter at Nettie's home in New York State.
Of course, the advent of two pretty and otherwise
attractive young ladies in a town like G——

awakened considerable curiosity and interest.
They were invited out, feasted and entertained by
the ladies of the town to a degree almost dangerous; dangerous, provided they had been frivolous
young maidens, which they were not. Their heads
were not easily turned, nor their hearts ready to
be stormed; therefore, at the end of their gay season, they were as fresh, as vivacious, as sensible
and free from guile as when they began it. Their
close friendship served to guard them from society's
contagious evils, for they acted, one for the other,
as guardian and consort. Nettie not having a
brother or sister of her own, naturally clung to
Belle with greater affection. Her uncle's son,
Roger, had left his home some years before, after
a brief but serious quarrel with his father, and had
never returned; in fact, he had not even written.

Nettie had become very much attached to this
boy; but as time passed she but vaguely remembered the circumstances connected with his departure, for her uncle seldom spoke of him in her
presence. Roger had been quick-tempered, but
Nettie had loved him sincerely, and he, in boy
fashion, had amply returned her affection, showing
his fondness for her in the thousand ways of which
children are so capable.

The recollection of one particular event was
stamped indelibly upon her memory. She had
one morning entered a small garden near her

uncle's house in girlish thoughtlessness, when, to
her surprise and horror, there appeared before her
a savage dog of huge proportions. Growling
fiercely, and showing its wicked teeth, it followed
her to a corner of the garden where it viciously
stood guard over her, not allowing her to move a
step. She had reached a condition of fright known
only to those timid natures who have been simi-
larly situated, when her cousin Roger happened
to look out of an upper window of Mr. Dexter's
house and saw the trouble. In less time than it
takes to tell it, he was down in the garden vigorously belaboring, with a large poker, the brute,
who, not relishing that sort of treatment, and suc-
cumbing quickly to the sovereignty of man and
poker, went howling down the street, never, it is
to be hoped, to return. Roger ever after this was
Nettie's hero. A mutual admiration syndicate was
started, which, until Roger's departure, tied the
knot of their childish fealty to one another tighter
and stronger than ever before. There was, therefore, a tender spot cherished in Nettie's heart for
this absent, excommunicated one, which time was
unable to eradicate.

The young men upon Cup Island were awakened
with the early day on Tuesday morning by a lusty
voice shouting, " Hello ! Is there anybody to
hum ?" accompanying the question with a lively
banging upon the door of the cottage. Jack was

the first to awake, and, stepping quickly to the window, said, with some anxiety,—

"What's the row down there? Who is it? What do you want? Oh, is that you, Mr. Sandy? Good-morning. Hold on a jiffy, and I will be down to let you in."

Tom rolled lazily over, and, gradually gaining consciousness, asked Jack, in a sleepy sort of way, if there were burglars about.

"Yes," said Jack, hastily donning his outer garments. "Don't you hear them whistling?"

Sure enough, "The Fisher's Hornpipe" came floating in through the open window, accompanied by a tattoo upon the door which would have aroused the admiration of a drum-major. Jack ran down and admitted the drummer.

"I've fetched ye over them things," said he, picking up a basket, carrying it into the house, and returning for a large tin pail filled with milk. "I reckon 'twould be better to lower that butter down into the well, fur it gits tolable hot here daytimes, an' it might run away from ye."

"No; we don't git a night-mail in Oldport," in answer to a question from Jack, who then asked,—

"What time do you open the post-office in the morning, Mr. Sandy?"

"Waal, long about eight o'clock, ef I happen to be thar at the store. I hev a young feller to open the store at six o'clock, while I'm doin' up my

chores. Good-morning, Dorkter. Hope you had
a good night's rest, sir. Fair night for sleepin';
good sea-breeze, an' no skeeters."

"Do you have mosquitoes at Oldport, Sam?"
asked Tom, quickly.

"Waal, they is times, Dorkter, yer know," said
Sandy, scratching his head meditatively, and seeing his mistake,—"they is times when the tarnal
critters will swarm everywhere, and I s'pose Oldport ain't no 'ception; but yer needn't be afeered
of the ole lady gittin' bit, for my spouse hez net-
tin' up to every winder in the shanty. The raskils
never tackle me. I like to hear 'em sing of a
night, but my wife's dreadful sensitive at 'em; an'
when she's bit they swell up big as a hen's egg,
and pester her all day long with their itchin'. I
reckon I'll be 'round with that boat 'bout noon-
time," he continued, forgetting the mosquitoes.
" I'm going down now to git some of the boys to
help me launch her an' see how she rides. Yer
see, I've been heavy-plankin' her inside, and I
want ter see how she rides when I git her new
ballus' in. Oh, she isn't a bit cranky. Don't
you be skeered. Only I want her to look kind
o' ship-shape an' snug, so's the ladies won't be
ashamed on her. Do yer understan' sailin' a
craft, Dorkter?"

"Somewhat," said Tom, winking at Jack.

"I reckoned yer did, fur yer father was as neat

a sailor fur a lan'-lubber as ever I seen. I allus calkerlated he hed taken a vige when he was a youngster somewhor. He had a keen eye fur ducks, too; so don't forget it. An' he was a good hand at a gun, an' knew which end was dangerous. Like as not yer friend is a banker?" nodding his head in Jack's direction, who, at the other end of the room, was taking the things out of the basket.

"Oh, no," said Tom.

"Lawyer, maybe?" said Sandy, in a tone which struggled in vain to sound indifferent.

"No," said Tom; "he is not a lawyer, exactly."

"What may he do fur a livin', then?" asked Sandy, getting desperate, but determined.

"He is a student of chiaroscuro and perspective," said Tom, in his most impressive manner.

This reply seemed to perfectly satisfy Sandy, who, with a grunt of approval, prepared to depart, saying that he would return in the middle of the day with the sail-boat.

A few days after this they heard through Mrs. Tillottson, who had gathered it from some of the villagers, that Sandy had told several of them that Jack was soon to be some kind of a doctor, for Dr. Tillottson had informed him that he (Jack) was studying to be a "curious-curer." He also said openly that, for his part, he didn't take much stock in these new-fangled doctors, who pretended

to cure by "rubbin' an' 'lectrics, an' all such perspectives."

It may be supposed from this that Mr. Sandy
was not an intelligent man, but quite the contrary
was the case. His knowledge was to a large extent—in fact, almost exclusively—of the practical
kind. If a horse in the village or neighborhood
was sick or disabled, Mr. Sandy's veterinary skill
was sure to be called upon, and generally by no
means in vain. If an arm was broken, and the
village doctor was out of town; if a potato crop
was in danger, if a cow obstinately refused to
"give down," if hens could not be coaxed to lay,
or if a pump would not do its duty, our friend
Sandy could generally suggest a remedy which
proved effective. Among the villagers he was a
sort of Solomon, a man for emergencies. When,
therefore, his proclamation went abroad, giving
Jack such a reputation for mysticism as was in-
volved in his mysterious words "curious-curer,"
"perspectives," and "'lectrics," it is not strange
that they should have lifted him, in their minds,
up to the level of things marvellous and unac-
countable. Of this Jack had frequent evidence
during his stay in the neighborhood. Jack's costume, on his sketching jaunts, by no means led to
a lessening of this feeling. He often wore a white
helmet (not so common in this country then as
now, an excellent head-protector from the sun's

rays), a jersey and pants of some very light-colored material, probably corduroy, and his feet were encased in a pair of white-canvas tennis shoes. Add to this costume a figure seventy-three inches in height from heel to crown, with a weight of graceful correspondence, a beard light-brown in color and of German type, close-cut hair, and a habit of walking very erect, and we have Jack as he appeared to people more or less accustomed to the sight of summer tourists or tennis players. How he appeared to these simple villagers may perhaps be best described by quoting the words of one of the village matrons, who was describing him to farmer Green, her good husband.

"Well, yer see, Abner, I was fearful took back. I sot thar a milkin' the yaller brindle clus by the woods in the corner of the old south pasture, where I allus milks her, when I heerd some one a-comin' long the road whistlin'. I looked up, and thar was a great tall feller all in white, jest as Jim Parsons would look with nothing but his underclothes on, and a sort of scoop thing a settin' on top of his head, an' a pair of white slippers on his feet, inside out. I knew in a minit it was that curious-curer chap, an' almost giggled right out in his face. Pretty soon he came right close up ter me an' leaned over the rails, an' said good-mornin', so cheerful-like that I felt kind of ashamed o' myself for laughin' at him. He looked smilin' enough, too; but, dear me, when

c   d   5

I fust seen him I thought 'twas Pete Briggs, the miller, gone crazy. He asked me a few questions which I managed to answer civil enough, though 'twas much as I could do ter keep from bu'stin' right out laughin', and all the time he was talkin' he was writin'—or I thought he was—something in a little book he took out of his pocket. Jest afore he went away, though, he showed me the book, an' thar was a picter of the woods, with the big chestnut which I wouldn't let you chop down last fall, an' thar was the yaller brindle a standin' by the fence, half asleep, an', as I live, thar was I myself, as nat'ral as life, a sittin' thar a milkin' the yaller brindle on that old starch-box. That feller ought to be a' artist or a photygrapher sure. It was killin'."

Tom's appearance did not seem at all strange to these people at Oldport. Tall and dark, with full side-whiskers and moustache, he wore a Scotch cap, a gray flannel shirt tucked in at the waist and confined by a leather belt, with dark pants tucked into high-top boots. His was a costume perfectly familiar to these fish-eating people; it smacked more of the true sailor.

After Sandy's departure, the young men busied themselves about breakfast, after which they began to make preparations for the arrival and reception of the girls the following day. They gathered running vines, went over to the village where they bought flags and fireworks, ransacked the woods back of Oldport for wild-flowers, and erected a flag-pole on the cottage. They trimmed the girls' part of the upper room with handsome vines, decorated the walls with flags, and placed wild-flowers in every available spot, so that from the bare and uninviting attic, the room was transformed into a bower of fragrant beauty. In the midst of their preparations they were interrupted by the arrival of Sandy with the sail-boat. Tom gave her a critical inspection as she rounded up to the little pier in the cove, expressing by his looks his satisfaction. Her name, "The Queen," in large but neat letters, was painted on her stern. She was large enough to comfortably accommodate six, or perhaps, on a pinch, eight or ten persons. She was sloop-rigged, carried a heavy sail, a light jib, and a centre-board. She was not a grey-hound in build or speed, but was a fast sailer, and admirably adapted for a safe pleasure-boat, capable of successfully coping with the variable winds and tides around the islands and along the coast near where she was built. She had a locker or small cabin forward, in which provisions, clothing, etc., could be stored, or in which, in case of an emer-gency, three or four people could stow themselves away quite comfortably.

Mr. Sandy was hypereulogistic in his praises of the craft, and insisted upon their immediately taking a little sail to prove his statements. This they proceeded to do; Tom stepping on board last, taking the tiller, and in a graceful and masterly manner catching a sail full of wind. After a few experiments in rounding the points of the island, in stemming the tide, and in tacking and beating up before the wind, they decided that she was a comfortable little boat, obedient to the helm, and comparatively easy to handle.

Thus amusing themselves in various ways, they pleasantly passed the second day of their sojourn upon Cup Island.

Wednesday morning dawned upon them bright and pleasant. They were up and moving long before Mr. Sandy appeared with the supplies. They had passed the previous night in the bunks, which Jack had constructed in a very creditable manner. They were nailed against the wall, one above the other, after the manner of those commonly seen upon steamboats, and, when provided with the bedding, which was brought from the apartment above, rendered good and comfortable service. By hanging up blankets they contrived to effectually partition off a sleeping apartment from the main room, and the effect was withal quite Oriental, if not unique. The village carpenter had partitioned off the upper room also, so that there were three small apartments instead of one large room.

When the time for the arrival of the train bearing the ladies drew near, the young men began to
exhibit symptoms of nervousness. Jack busied
himself improving the immediate surroundings
of the cottage, which he decorated here and there
with flags and bright colors, while Tom occupied
his time in preparing "The Queen" for their
reception.

Finally they left the island and sailed across to
Oldport, towing the row-boat behind them to carry
baggage on their return. They moored the boats
to the pier, and, hiring a many-seated wagon,
went to the railroad station, where they were soon
greeted by the whistling and rumbling of the
approaching train.

CHAPTER III.

A Story without a Hero—Two thoroughly American Young
Men—The Arrival of the Ladies—The Van Twists—The
Girls upon Bogus Island—Bid's Adventure—The Rescue—
Cup Island by Moonlight.

It is only fair to inform the reader that we
claim no hero to our little story. Tom and Jack
are both good enough fellows in their way. Generous, truthful, and kind-hearted, if you please, but
not perfect. In vain have we searched the cosmos

for a hero free from imperfection, an immaculate sort of individual, without a blemish to mar a character which the gods might envy. We do not mean to imply by this that we desired a goody-goody young gentleman in the sense commonly accepted, but that specimen of a high-minded, perfect-souled individual with *homo sum* written in letters of gold upon his physiognomy. A creature who breakfasts upon humility, dines upon probity, and sups with gusto upon self-denial,—a sort of modern example of self-abnegated purity. Our youngsters were none such. They were simply good-natured, honest men of the world, as men of the world go. Free from mean streaks, they would be sure to scorn an act which savored of pettiness. Perhaps a great emergency might bring out some act of self-forgetfulness which would suggest the heroic, but emergencies are not common nowadays, and we are content to present Tom and Jack to the reader as they are, below the average of heroes as heroes run in romance. With all their imperfections and shortcomings there was in their manner, in the frank expression of their eyes, an indescribable something, which so surely wins honest feminine regard and trusting confidence. Could we say more in their favor than this?

Such heroes, however, are not rare. America is full of them. They are not ideal; they are real.

They are not perfect, they are progressive; constantly improving under our precious feminine encouragement. They are not over-domestic, but their warm-heartedness on occasions brings out the nobleness of their natures, while there is nothing consistent with true gallantry which they will not readily do.

They do not sulk through a lifetime nursing a sick, torn heart which will not heal; for, once in love, they generally win the object of their choice by an irresistible tenacity of purpose, born, perhaps, of Puritan ancestry, or an essential outcome from the truthfulness and joyfulness of their natures. Another, and perhaps better reason for their success in affairs of the heart, is that there is nothing ephemeral or clandestine in their courtship. They are as sure of their loves as the magnet is of the steel. The net of the flirt has no charm for them; they play around it but never in it. In fact, they do not flirt themselves because of their instinctive honesty.

They are, to be sure, in one sense, evanescent, fond of a change, of merriment, a joke, of pleasures light; but these, like the anticipatory aromas of a fine dinner, are but the fleeting harbingers of something more substantial. In their respective professions our young men excelled, which was perhaps reason enough for their eligibility to the highest social circles in New York. We say the highest, meaning that element which if not at the top or head, by virtue of intelligence, was none the less considered the society, *par excellence distingué.* We do not mention this circumstance to emphasize their talents, although they were by no means mediocre; but simply to inform the reader of their social advantages. Like the majority of shining lights, they practised their handicrafts upon the very people among whom it was their privilege to shine; a fact in harmony, we think, with the laws which should govern social equity and equality. De Quincey, in his "Literary Reminiscences," has made the following interesting statement: "Three persons in all" (meaning in England) "may be mentioned from the ranks of intellectual people who have had a footing in privileged society. I mean not merely had admission there, but a known and extensive acceptation. These three were Lord Byron, Dr. Johnson, and Sir Walter Scott. Now it is observable that the first was in some sense a denizen of such society, in right of birth and rank, and of both the others it is remarkable that their passes were first countersigned by kings. Dr. Johnson's by George III., Sir Walter's by George IV."

Our young friends were not championed into society channels by any such methods. They fairly won their social spurs by efficiency, not only

in the practice of their talents as professional men,
but by their natural refinement in manners and in
matters of taste. It is, therefore, with a sense of
national pride that we introduce them to our
readers as typical Americans, if not as typical
heroes. They were both educated to look upon
work as honorable, and not with the pusillanimous
idea that idleness or the dawdling away time use-
lessly was the true insignia of nobility. Happiness was to them no *Ignis Fatuus*, it was life,
reality.

The train from the city steamed alongside of the
little station, at Oldport, exactly on time.

The passengers alighted, the trunks and other
baggage were thrown upon the wooden platform,
the whistle sounded, the bell tolled, and away
went the train gaining impetus with each throe
of the engine, leaving a flurry of dust, smoke, and
anxious passengers in its wake.

Tom recognized his mother and sister at once,
and, after the usual formal introductory overtures,
he and Jack succeeded in getting the females
safely seated in the long wagon, having made
arrangements with the station-agent to have the
trunks, etc., transferred to the town at once. Another party had alighted at the Oldport Station,—
an elderly gentleman, his wife and daughter and
servants,—but more of them anon.

" Here we are at last," said Belle, clapping her

hands as gleefully as a young child. "What a curious-looking place this always is! Why, where are our trunks? Oh, yes, I see them. Nettie, isn't this a queer town?"

"I see no houses to make it a town," said Nettie, laughing; "and where is the water?"

"You will see presently," said Tom, with a smile; "but first let us get under way. Hop in, Jack."

"All right," said Jack, suiting the action to the word, and, jumping in beside Belle, off they went.

The drive to Oldport proper was doubly pleasant to Jack, for he had an appreciative sharer of his enjoyment of the quaint scenery by the way, while Tom, with Nettie by his side on the front seat, drove the horses, occasionally directing a sly glance of admiration at the trim figure of his lovely neighbor.

"Are you familiar with country life, Miss Knowles?" Tom asked, at length.

"Yes and no," Nettie replied, pleased to enter into a conversation which she knew not how to begin. "Yes, because, as you remember, no doubt, our boarding-school was situated in the outskirts of a country town; and no, because, as perhaps you do not know, we were denied opportunities to enjoy what you probably mean by country life. But I love the country, and it cer-

tainly must be amusing and instructive to be able
to study the natures and manners of country
people, to say nothing of nature herself. Oh,
what a lovely view of the water !" The wagon
had ascended a slight eminence as they turned a
bend in the road.

"Yes," Tom replied, slackening the speed of
the horses; "and if you will look carefully between those two high trees on the right you will
see one end of Cup Island, our temporary home.
A little farther on to the right you will notice
Oldport, which is recognizable by the steeple of
the little white church."

"I think I can see the island, and—yes, there is
the church-steeple," said Nettie, turning immediately and imparting the information to Belle.
Chatting pleasantly in this manner, they were not
long in reaching Mr. Sandy's cottage, the quaint
color of which seemed to greatly amuse the ladies.

Mr. Sandy's reception of the party was a little
shy, but cordial.

Mrs. Tillottson was pleased with her new quarters, and seemed relieved that things had turned
out so auspiciously. Her sister seemed delighted
to come to her journey's end, and immediately
entered into a confidential chat with Mrs. Sandy.
It had been planned that they should all dine
at Mr. Sandy's, and soon after their arrival they
assembled at table. The girls were somewhat

surprised to find sitting opposite them the gentleman and his family they had previously noticed
upon the train.

"Mrs. Tillottson an' young ladies an' gents,"
said Sandy, clearing his throat with a mighty
effort, accompanied by a gracious wave of his
sunburned hand, "allow me ter interduce yer ter
Major Van Twist, Mrs. Van Twist, and their dar-
ter, from Forestville, Connecticut." After which
grandiloquent remark he subsided into his seat at
the head of the table.

"I am happy to meet you," said Mrs. Tillottson,
bowing to the Van Twists.

The major bowed cordially in return and arranged himself in true military style to reply, but
before he could command words Mrs. Van Twist
said,—

"Mr. Sandy informs me, madame, that your
young folks are to camp for a while on Cup
Island. It is somewhat strange, but very pleasant
and opportune, that we should both arrive to-day,
as the major, my daughter, and myself are about
to visit our cottage upon Smoke Island for a few
weeks."

"It will be very nice to have such near neighbors, I am sure," said Mrs. Tillottson, cheerfully.

"Why, that is jolly," said Tom, gayly. "It is,
indeed, a surprise, and a very agreeable one."

"We come here almost every summer," said

Miss Van Twist, "except when mamma insists upon going abroad. For my part I would always prefer coming here; it is so stupid, rushing about on the continent from one hotel to another like some restless travelling agent, especially when we cannot understand a word that people say. Then, too, the people here are so very amusing; such a queer set."

All this was said directly at Tom, who appeared to listen intently while wondering to himself how the girls would get on with this forward creature who seemed to delight so in the sound of her own voice. Then noticing that Mr. Sandy was apparently about to resent her slighting remarks about the Oldport people, he said quickly, addressing her mother,—

"Mrs. Van Twist, if we, that is Mr. Stratton and myself, can be of service at any time to you during your stay upon Smoke Island, I trust you will command us, and I am sure it will give us great pleasure."

"Yes," said Jack, in his dry, pleasing way; "the doctor and I are both excellent cooks, and as a housemaid with an enviable character I most confidently recommend my services; provided you have set tubs and the modern conveniences, and give me Thursdays and Sundays out."

This sally brought a smile to all faces and a roar from the major. His wife alone maintained a serious demeanor, being one of those peculiarly-constituted individuals who concentrate their mental forces so thoroughly upon the realities of life that they cannot by any moderate effort descend to side issues.

Then Belle, feeling that conciliation might be in order, said, addressing Mrs. Van Twist,—

" Mr. Stratton and my brother have been keeping bachelor's hall for several days at the cottage upon Cup Island, and no doubt feel themselves capable, even with this limited experience, of solving the most intricate problems in domestic economy."

Here she cast a mischievous glance at Jack, who, not to be put down and ready for fun, replied,—

" Yes, we have made a complete success of it, as our ability to invite such distinguished guests for a prolonged visit will testify. We desire them to witness our complete triumph."

"And capture your colors," said Nettie, laughing, who was now wrought up to a conversational pitch. "We have planned a campaign, which, in the end, you will be as ready to admire as you are now perhaps likely to ignore."

"And we mean to fight it out on that line if it takes all summer," said Belle, hiding her laughing mouth behind a glass of water.

The major enjoyed the controversy immensely.

" If there must be war," he said, swelling up, as he always did when he began to speak, " if there must be war, I am from this moment a willing volunteer, and will join the forlorn hope. We will storm Cup Island together, young ladies."

" Well," said Tom, looking curiously at Nettie, " if you capture Cup Island by storm, do not forget that you first landed upon its hospitable shores as guests and in the welcome summer sunshine."

" I have heard," said Jack, persistently, " of storming ' rock-ribbed' fortresses and capturing hearts by siege, but who ever heard of storming Paradise or Parnassus or Cup Island by assault ?"

" In a storm, *a salt* might do it," said Tom, perpetrating a vicious pun.

" Don't be alarmed, ladies," said Jack; " if the doctor is unwell he can cure himself."

" Thank you," said Tom ; " I feel better already. And now, if the ladies will excuse us, perhaps we had better transport their luggage over to the aforesaid paradise."

" No, indeed," said Belle ; " Nettie and I will go over first with you, and then you can return for the things; we are dying to inspect the island."

" All right, then," Tom replied. " Follow me and behold *Nirvanna.*"

The whole party went to see them off at the pier, and they were soon scudding across the water under full sail, Tom at the helm. Jack stood upon the bowsprit flourishing his hat at those upon shore, the two girls made a display of linen handkerchiefs, and Bid sat near the stern with her lap and arms literally buried in wraps and wearing apparel. It had been arranged for Bid to stay upon the island with them and do the heavy work.

Their brilliant reception at the island was a delightful surprise to the young ladies. Jack and the doctor entered spiritedly into the thing, singing a song of welcome to banjo accompaniment, setting off fire-crackers, and delivering neat speeches of welcome, in which they dwelt enthusiastically upon the distinguished characters and rare virtues of the new arrivals and the priceless advantages of their new Eldorado.

After this was all accomplished to their satisfaction, the young men started back to Oldport for the luggage; and the girls, delighted at being left alone upon the island, immediately began an exploring expedition. They visited every nook and corner from North Rock to the summer-house upon Bogus Island. With this latter place they were delighted, and the tide being low they crossed the little cove with ease upon the boulders, which were hardly wet with the advancing tide, Belle carrying her sketch-book and Nettie her writing materials, leaving Bid at the cottage to fix things up and prepare supper.

Belle was soon interested in sketching an old wreck, which lay upon a reef, and was visible at low tide; while Nettie, after a brief indulgence in revery, busied herself in writing a long letter to Mr. Dexter, her uncle, to whom the news of her removal to Oldport would be fresh. Thus occupied, time sped unawares, until Belle, looking at last at her watch, discovered that it was after five o'clock.

"Why, Nettie," she exclaimed, surprised; "I did not dream it so late. We must return to the cottage."

Nettie acquiesced, and gathering up their things they started to return; but here a difficulty stared them in the face, and both stood upon the shore of the cove puzzled, irresolute, and astonished. Bogus Island was now a genuine island, and they were completely surrounded by water. The tide had "stolen a march" on them while they were enjoying themselves in the summer-house. They were prisoners. What to do they did not know. Belle, with a face paling with fright, turned to Nettie, and in a trembling voice said,—

"Nettie, what *shall* we do? Let's scream."

"No," said Nettie, thinking of the young men. "They will think us great geese if we do."

"Can we not wade across?" said Belle, in tones of despair.

"But suppose they were to return and find us

e   6*

wading like a couple of veritable herons, we would never hear the last of it," said Nettie, with a grim smile.

Nettie's coolness, and the facetious vein of her last remark, somewhat restored Belle's equanimity at least temporarily.

Meantime, what had become of Jack and the doctor? They had reached Oldport shortly after leaving the girls, and Tom, anxious to receive his mail, had been up to the post-office, where he learned that the afternoon train which bore the mail was delayed by an accident, a freight train having jumped the track, causing an impediment, which for an hour or so would obstruct all travel. Returning to the boat, they decided that instead of waiting they would take a short sail along the coast, perhaps catch a few blue-fish for breakfast, then return to Oldport for the mail and the balance of the luggage.

When they had sailed for about an hour due east the wind died completely down, making their immediate return impossible. Thus they were compelled to wait until it freshened up again, which it did not do for nearly three hours, making the time nearly seven o'clock before they arrived again at the Oldport pier.

The girls returned to the summer-house with long faces. The tide was rising rapidly, and rushing waters swiftly swept between the two islands, now rendering wading impossible. There were no signs of the young men, and they both admitted that their situation was somewhat ludicrous.

"What do you suppose keeps them?" said Belle, with a decided tremulousness in her voice.

"Something unexpected has delayed them," said Nettie, striving to be brave. "Perhaps they found that some of the baggage was missing and have driven over to the station for it. In that case they would hardly have returned by this time."

Thus, occasionally cheering each other, the two girls waited, communing with their thoughts, and listening to the noise of the rushing waters as they dashed against the rocks, the tide growing higher and higher.

They were in full view of the cottage, and Belle, whose eyes had been absently fixed upon it, suddenly saw Bid appear at the door and look in their direction.

"There is Bid!" she quickly exclaimed. "Let us wave our handkerchiefs and she will come to us."

This they did; but Bid, mistaking their signals of distress for a friendly salute, simply flourished a towel which was in her hand and disappeared within the cottage.

"Oh, dear!" said Belle; "how provoking;" then screaming at the top of her voice, "Bid! oh-h-h Bid! Come here quick, we want you!"

No response, however, came from headquarters,

for the distance was too great for Belle's voice to travel, and the wind was blowing toward them from that direction.

Presently, though, Bid appeared again, this time walking directly toward them with her calico dress thrown up over the back of her head, which the wind formed into a sort of balloon. Suddenly she paused, and the girls could hardly refrain from laughing as they saw the look of horror upon her face, when, on reaching the shore, she noticed the rushing water between them.

" Bid !" screamed Belle, " where *is* Tom ?"

"Oh, moi, moi! Oh, moi!" shouted Bid, across the cove. "Shure he's not back at all; but how did ye's get over the wather, anyhow ?"

" The tide was low," said Belle.

" The toide, was it ?" said Bid.

" Yes," said Belle, " the tide; but now it has risen and caught us here. Bid, what shall we do ?"

They shouted at Bid thus for perhaps half an hour; meantime Belle's watch showed that it was after seven o'clock, and the sun was declining rapidly behind the western hills of Connecticut. Bid, who was nearly wild with fright at the apparent danger of these two young ladies, who, to her simple mind, were in her sole charge, spied at last the little row-boat moored to a stake near her on the shore, where it had been left by the young men. In a moment she had made up her mind to rescue her dear girls at the risk of her own life; and before they were at all aware of her intentions, she had untied the painter, pulled the little boat toward her, stepped into it, and with the wrong end of an oar was wildly trying to impel the boat toward them. But poor Bid's skill did not correspond to her noble impulse. Unfortunately, in the methods of navigation her education had been wofully neglected, and this was her first attempt to manage a row-boat. As soon, therefore, as the boat floated out from the shore far enough to catch the strong flow of the tide, Bid and boat were swiftly swept away from between the islands, turning around and around in their uncertain course like a feather in the wind.

The girls by this time were really alarmed, for here was their last hope drifting away from them. They screamed all sorts of directions at Bid, who, apparently oblivious to everything they said, was frantically dashing the oar to and fro, which, like a straw in her brawny arms, splashed the water in every direction, particularly her own.

"Put the oar in the row-lock!" yelled Nettie, who was herself a tolerable sailor.

"Sit down on the seat or you will tip over!" screamed Belle. "Oh, dear! she don't hear a word."

"Bid!" screeched Nettie, at the top of her voice.

This seemed to attract her attention, for the poor woman ceased her struggles with the elements and turned toward them a face as long and woebegone as possible.

" Sit down !" Nettie continued, in the same high key.

Bid sat down, but with a narrow escape from capsizing.

" Now, Bid, sit still; you are going with the tide toward the shore; when you get near enough you can scream and attract the attention of people on the shore ;" but by this time Bid was out of distinct hearing, and both Nettie and Belle were thoroughly alarmed. Fortunately, Bid continued to sit still. Let us credit her with so much good judgment. She probably began to realize her nautical incompetency, and subdued her pride by ruminating upon the frailty of man when subjected to a conflict with the raging elements. She was now on thorough exhibition. Occasionally her Hibernian profile was presented to the girls,—her low forehead, short but by no means straight nose, large, strong lower jaws, and prominent lips, forcing her true pedigree upon them; then her full, mournful, scared face would drift into view, causing their tender hearts to ache for her, until at last her broad, large-waisted back forcibly reminded them of her native ability for endurance; and thus slowly revolving, like the dressed wax

figure in a dressmaker's window, she was gradually drifting away.

Tom and Jack meantime had just landed on the
opposite shore of the island, and were conveying
their first load of things to the cottage in some
haste, as clouds were forming and mounting in the
west, and they were expecting a thunder-shower.
They were surprised to find the cottage empty.
They knocked upon the wall, thinking that the
girls were up-stairs; they shouted, but in vain; and
finally, after assuring themselves that the cottage
was deserted, they wandered out upon the island,
where they immediately spied them in the summer-
house on Bogus Island.

But the girls did not return their looks. Their
gaze was riveted in another direction; they were
intently looking shoreward. The young men followed the direction of their glances, and then, for
the first time, saw poor Bid sitting in the little boat,
her face toward its bow, with an oar lying helplessly across her lap; while the boat, with its bow
six inches out of water, for Bid was sitting on the
rear seat, was slowly revolving on its keel as ma-
jestically as a balloon in mid-air.

"Hello!" shouted Jack and Tom in a breath,
both running at the same time toward Bogus
Island.

"Oh, Tom!" screamed Belle, when they were
within hearing distance. "Come quick, we have

been imprisoned for hours; but first save poor
Bid; save dear old Bid first!"

"Yes, yes," said Nettie, "do save Bid first."

Both young men were by this time doubled up
with laughter. They were convulsed. Now, your
true heroes would, of course, have dashed reck-
lessly into the billowy deep, breasted the angry
waves, and rescued the beautiful maidens at the
imminent risk of their own sweet lives; but Jack
and the doctor, as we have before stated, were not
true heroes. They did nothing of the sort. They
laughed, and the girls were somewhat reassured
by their hilarity, for their good sense told them
that the young men knew what they were about,
and would not have shown so much amusement
in the presence of actual danger.

"Boots," said Tom, as soon as he could command his voice sufficiently, "keep cool and we
will be back in a minute." Then hastening with
Jack over to "The Queen," they quickly cast her
off and were briskly sailing after the nautical
domestic in a good breeze.

Bid rescued, which was a matter soon accomplished, Tom took her place in the little boat and
pulled vigorously for Bogus Island, leaving Jack
to pilot "The Queen."

At this time great drops of rain began to fall,
the sky darkened rapidly, thunder rumbled in the
distance, and the wind, which hitherto had been

warm and moderate, increased to a stiff cool breeze which blew the spray from the tops of the small waves in the harbor. Jack returned safely to Cup Island with Bid, while Tom rowed lightly over the waves against the tide, having the strong wind in his favor. The girls, by the time he reached them, were thoroughly wet, the summer-house proving a poor protection in such a gale; but they were happy in the knowledge of Bid's safety, and in the assurance of Tom's powers. To bundle them into the boat, shove the boat across the cove, and land them upon the other shore took Tom but a short time; but the rain was now descending in torrents; and the loud cracking and booming thunder, preceded by vivid flashes of lightning, by no means reassured them of complete safety. Tom quickly moored the boat, then running after the girls, who were by this time half way to the cottage, he threw his coat over Nettie, who was the least protected. They were soon safely housed, looking like a brood of very wet chickens.

Their drenching did them no harm, for the air was not very cold, but bracing. The young ladies, rejoicing in the happy termination of their exciting adventure, were soon in high spirits, and at supper, having changed their apparel, a stranger could not have perceived that anything had occurred to interfere with their serenity.

"I told you we would capture the island by storm," said Belle, gayly.

"Which island?" asked Jack, roguishly; then added quickly, "I notice by your cheeks, ladies, that you have fulfilled your threat regarding colors."

Bid, who with her customary stoical indifference, was now ready to wait upon table, was asked by the doctor how she enjoyed her sail.

"Ah, Misther Torm," said she, "shure an' were it not for you and your good friend, it's the loikes av me wud now be tossin' at the bottom av the moanin' say."

Bid could not break herself of the habit of addressing the doctor as "Misther Torm." She had been in the family many years. She was a faithful soul, and ever after the event which had just happened, she held to the idea that Tom and Jack had saved her from the "moanin' say." Perhaps they had, who knows? The storm, which was now fiercely raging outside, had already lashed the waters of the harbor into angry waves, which in such a gale might easily have capsized the frail boat and its restless occupant, and Bid was less skilled in the natatorial science than in that of navigation; therefore, perhaps, she was not unreasonably grateful.

The young ladies also felt a true sense of security and comfortableness in the presence of Tom and Jack, while the beating of the rain upon the windows, the occasional lurid flashes of lightning, and the roar of the elements outside, added to their feeling of safety, as they enjoyed the warmth of the burning logs which crackled and blazed upon the hearth. They were brought, too, into closer acquaintanceship with the young men by the little adventure just related, which, of course, effected more in advancing their social intimacy than a whole week's residence upon the island might under ordinary circumstances have done.

The girls chatted incessantly and without restraint. They talked of their adventure, of the conveniences and inconveniences of the cottage which was to be their home, of their plans for enjoyment on Cup Island, of their school experiences, in fact of everything that seemed to pop into their young noddles; while the young men, delighted with such pleasant companionship, listened intently, now and then dropping an encouraging word, or giving a nod of approval, or deftly putting a question to draw forth more of such delicious eloquence.

They were a contented party; and now while they still talk the fierce wind gradually dies away, the heavy clouds pass to the south, and the soft rays of the mid-summer moon light up the scene outside with a sweet, mellow brilliancy. Cup

Island sparkles with a thousand crystal reflections, and peacefully yet regally holds her head high above the still troubled waters of the sound.

CHAPTER IV.

John Beesford Stratton—Character Comparisons—Jack's Letter to Bob Evans—Belle and Nettie gather Sea-Mosses, and are left by the Tide—Mr. Craik—Another Rescue—In Tow.

JACK STRATTON, or John Beesford Stratton at pleasure, was in many respects a genius. He was, in the first place, a natural born artist. There are those, we know, who deny such a possibility, claiming that all talent or power of accomplishment is acquired by cultivation. Nevertheless, we know that Jack, even as a very young child, evinced a strong natural, and without doubt, an inherited tendency toward art. We will therefore side with the phrenologists, for he unmistakably displayed a natural capacity for the artistic, and at a very tender age. He also possessed a nature pervaded by an apparently inexhaustible · current of good humor. Craniology may here again lay claim, for Jack's head certainly did have a jolly cast. It was a head to caress, like that of a faithful dog. A tender heart may be added to

the attributes mentioned, and we have in Jack
Stratton a man whose life was certain to be a
happy one; a person in whose nature there was
no room for the world's perplexities or for anxiety
about the morrow. Genial, well-bred, well-read,
an experienced traveller, communicative, yet a
good listener, handsome and young. What more
could be asked? He was also a well-tempered
youth, and had been safely through those inevitable fires of experience which either make or ruin
a man. In his case the metal left the furnace
brighter and purer for the smelting.

Beneath that halo of good nature which always
seemed to surround him, there was a groundwork
of discrimination, and for so young a man, a notably wise and discreet judgment. His love for the
doctor was deep-rooted. In him he saw a nature
true as steel; and Tom returned his friendship
measure for measure. Their characters, however,
were very dissimilar. Tom, while he enjoyed a
frolic as a sort of recreation or refreshment, had
his serious moments,—moments when the intricate and perplexing problems of life seemed to
flow into and flood his soul with anxious thought.
His tastes, too, were different; where Jack saw
beauty, Tom found a background of true moral
worth. Jack saw form; Tom substance. But
this difference in their methods of receiving the
world's impressions served to draw their natures

into a closer and more sympathetic companionship, for what one lacked the other possessed and
yielded freely.

Their methods were different, but were at the
same time complementary. They were by different processes possessed of affectionate dispositions.
Jack's moods were spontaneous, while Tom's affections seemed latent, always ready present, a matter
of permanency, an instinctive possession. The
knowledge which Stratton gained of men was
borne to him through his keen artistic vision. He
was what Lavater would have called a natural
physiognomist. Tom judged human nature by a
different standard; he weighed mankind in the
scales of thoughtful comparison. Jack took fan-
cies and dislikes at sight ; Tom only by lengthened
acquaintance. Jack lived almost entirely in the
present, while Dr. Tillottson revered the past, re-
joiced in the present, and reasoned upon the
future. Yet with all these differences they were
alike. Both were enthusiastic in their respective
professions, both unselfish in their aspirations.
They worked from a love of results, not recom-
pense. Jack sketched and painted because he
took pleasure in reproducing the wonders of nature, discovering with each progressive step in his
work something new to admire. The doctor
healed the sick and relieved suffering humanity
because he loved to do good. This zealous un-

selfishness served to make them popular with
their patrons, and was also instrumental in making
them more skilful in the practice of their professions. Thus at heart they were affinities.

After a few days upon Cup Island, Jack, who
had been busily active every moment of the time,
remembered that he had promised to write to an
intimate friend in the city, one Robert Evans, a
brother artist. Evans was a young man about
Jack's age. They had studied together in Florence under the same master, and had renewed
their intimacy in New York, to their mutual advantage, for both gave good promise of becoming
famous. They were both looked upon with favor-
ing eyes by that portion of the great public who
take more than a passing interest in the specialty
of painting. Evans was a frequent visitor at Jack's
den, as he called it, where the three young men
enjoyed many happy hours in social chat and
festive communion.

To Evans, then, Jack, after some struggling for
opportunity, wrote the following amusing letter:

"DEAR BOB,—Nothing is more difficult, as you
are probably well aware for an artist, than to pause
in his mad career to indite a letter; but just a few
words must I write to Bobbie, if only to say 'how
d'ye,' or 'God bless you.' Ah, my lad, I am very
happy,—I may say supremely so,—and if I had

you within ear-reach, I should be strongly tempted to tell you the cause of my joy. But you must not ask me. Silence! I'm mum. No, no, though, this won't do; on reflection, Robert, I relent; you deserve better treatment at my hands and can be trusted. Were we not together nurtured in that cradle of art, Florence? and does not our mother-muse smile benignly upon us as twin daubers? Indeed, I should be conscience-smit did I not share my joys with you as readily as I would my sorrows. Know ye, then, that the cause of all my present felicity is a woman. Now down on your knees. She is an angel.

> Why do I love this lassie so?
> This bonnie bit of a girl,
> With golden hair, and eyes as fair
> As the blue in the heart of a pearl.

"By the way, Bobbie, it is essential that you should understand that the heart of a pearl is unmistakably blue.

"You will be somewhat astonished when I inform you that our party at the cottage here on Cup Island has grown from two to five individuals, and more surprised when I inform you that the three additional individuals are of the female persuasion. It happened in this way:

"Tom's mother, being out of health, has sought the sea-air at Oldport, where she, with her sister, is comfortably established. Her daughter, Miss Belle, and a friend, Miss Knowles, came on with them. Tom's sister urged him to allow her, with her friend, to stop at the cottage with him; so here we are, four of us, as jolly a crowd as you will seldom meet. 'Bid,' Mrs. Tillottson's maid, is with us, and makes an excellent cook. She has the ancestral atmosphere of burnt peat about her, is Hibernian to the core, both in brogue and blarney, and is withal an indispensable institution. Miss Knowles is a beauty. Tom's sister, Belle, is divine. I mean it. We have now been but two days together, yet the gavel has fallen, and I'm a goner. I cannot write about anything else. Of course she don't suspect; neither does Tom, dear old chap, and I can't seem to muster up courage enough to tell him what a terrible fix I am in. What *shall* I do, Bobbie? Send me some fatherly advice. I have tried my level best to throw off the spell and laugh myself out of it, but it is no use. There is a sweet melody playing constantly upon my heart-strings which I cannot and will not interrupt, for it attunes the routine of my life to a harmony, which stimulates me to better hopes and deeds; and should it cease, or should discord intrude, I fear I could not bear the strain. But I must be a man, and write something of what is happening hereabouts.

" There is another little island—Smoke Island—

f

within a stone's throw of us, on which live for the
summer a Major Van Twist, wife and daughter,
with a small retinue of three servants. The major
is a jolly chappie, rather below the medium height
and above the ordinary breadth,—what we call, in
broad English, stocky. He is a good sort of a
fellow, who smokes prime Havanas, and is given
to forty-rod puns. His wife, who, I understand,
brought the major an immense fortune on their
wedding-day, is one of the queer sort. You know,
Bobbie,—one of those peculiar females who think
a great deal of their standing and very little of
their letters. She drops an occasional g, and is a
wholesale dealer in superlatives. I haven't gauged
the daughter yet, but she would sit for a splendid
Goddess of Liberty. They have a luxurious cottage on Smoke Island, which rather throws our
modest affair in the shade. We have the good
times, though. Yesterday a large yacht anchored
in Oldport Harbor, and the gentlemen are now
visiting the Van Twists; friends of theirs, I suppose. Tom says that the yacht looks like that of
Van Dusen, the millionaire,—he that paid me the
snug price last year for the Beatrice picture, you
know. If it is he, and he finds me out, he will
be over here, I suppose. There are four in their
party, and one is dark enough to be a Spaniard.
Here comes Tom again, and he says the yacht is
the 'Siren' (Van Dusen's, you know). Tom says

he just made out the name with the glass, and that Van Dusen is related to the Van Twists.

"I am sketching a fine old wreck here, and intend to work up a picture out of it for the exhibition, if I am not too much of a wreck myself. Meantime, I see a certain face in everything I look at.

"There is an abundance of material scattered about here for good work,—odds and ends, you know; queer-looking farm-houses, with the high, old-fashioned gable roofs ; eccentric characters, etc. Yesterday we passed a boatload of fishermen just landing a net. Some of them had on red shirts, and their sea-dog faces warm-tinted by the sun—then low in the western sky, which made a gorgeous play of red upon the dripping net and waters—was a sight which will haunt my memory until I make one of my futile attempts to reproduce it.

"We have two boats,—a sloop-rigged and a row-boat. The exercise of rowing is fine, and we are all benefited by it greatly. Tom looks like a veteran tar already. I enclose a rough sketch of him, and likewise a profile view of his sister. Is it not a wonderful face ? I caught the expression on the sly while she was eagerly watching a sea-gull catch a fish.

"By the way, Bob, please go to White's, the fruit-store on the corner, and tell Mr. White to send me a basket of his best peaches every week. *She* likes them. And will you be kind enough, old boy, to send me Scribble's last novel? *She* has heard of it. I know you too well, Bobbie, to fear that these commissions will trouble you.

"Write soon to

"Your humble friend,

"JACK."

The day following the writing of this epistle the girls, who understood rowing, took the little boat with the intention of making a short visit upon Mrs. Tillottson, in order to carry her some fresh fish of their own catching. After this visit they had planned to row along the coast and gather sea-mosses for pressing.

The day was perfect; too warm perhaps inland, but on the water, breeze enough was stirring to make the air comfortable and invigorating.

After seeing Mrs. Tillottson, presenting their gift of fish, and receiving an assurance from Mrs. Sandy that the fish should be cooked with due care, they left Oldport, and half drifted and half rowed along the coast with the tide until they came to a sloping, sandy beach, with here and there a cluster of huge black rocks. The tide was going out, which was favorable for their pursuit, so running the boat ashore they were soon briskly engaged in searching among the rocks and all along the beach for mosses.

In their enthusiasm they had failed to notice behind a clump of rocks, near their landing-place, another boat about the size of their own. Half sitting, half reclining in the boat was a man. A Panama hat was drawn down over his eyes, but enough of his features were visible to show that he was handsome. His complexion was dark enough to suggest Spanish blood, which idea was not lessened by the appearance of his small shapely feet and well-formed, effeminate hands. His dress was jaunty, and not free from an attempt at show, but it fitted a figure, the pleasing proportions of which would redeem almost any inconsistency of cut or quality. At first glance the very boat itself seemed to borrow dash and buoyancy from its occupant. There are individuals who, until we know them and have weighed their character, seem to lend beauty or grace to whatever they draw near to or touch by their perfection of manner and figure.

Such a person was this man; and as he now sits erect and pushes back his hat, we see a face so pervaded by the lines of beauty that we involuntarily admire. A dark, symmetrically curled moustache covers his upper lip, and handsome regular teeth are brought in sight as he murmurs something to himself. Let us listen to his words:

8

"What an idiot I was to leave New York to coop myself up in that jackass's yacht. I ought to have known better. They say he is a millionaire, but devil take him, he won't stake anything. I tried him last night again by all the arts I possess, and after toddy, too; but he won't drink much, and a straight game of euchre is all he seems to care or know anything about, and not a d—— cent would he stake on the game. As for the others they are N.G. One a parson with his prayer-meetings and gibberish, and the other with nothing to talk about but bugs and fish, and such nonsense. If I didn't think it might lead to something rich I would skip back to New York and leave the whole crowd. I wonder what keeps Van Dusen so long. He said he was only going up to that farm-house on an errand and would be back in ten minutes. He has been away now nearly an hour."

He now stood up in the boat in order to get an unobstructed view of the farm-house. As he did so he saw Van Dusen a short distance from him on the beach in conversation with two young ladies. Stepping quickly out of the boat he walked leisurely toward them. Van Dusen saw him approaching, and, when near enough, said with a gracious wave of the hand in his direction,—

"Ladies, allow me to introduce my friend, Mr. Craik."

Then in turn introducing the ladies to Mr. Craik, he continued,—

"You have arrived most opportunely, for we must assist in delivering these ladies from rather an unfortunate dilemma. They have been gathering mosses along the shore, and during their absence their boat has been left high and dry by the tide."

"Certainly, it will give me great pleasure to be of service to the ladies," said Craik, with one of his fascinating smiles.

"No, no," he continued, "please do not exert yourself." This to Belle, who offered to help them with the boat. "We can easily do it alone."

They soon pushed the boat over the deep sand into the water, and Craik, stepping into it, guided it alongside of a flat rock from which it was easy for the girls to embark. Thanking the gentlemen for their kindness, the girls, who were now safely seated, took up the oars and were soon industriously pulling for home.

"How strange," said Belle, presently, "that we should meet them here, and in such a plight. What a handsome man that Mr. Craik is. He is certainly the best looking and most graceful man I ever saw."

Nettie was silent, but presently she said, quietly,—

"He certainly is very good looking, but there is something about him which I do not like; I can-

not describe it, and perhaps if I had met him alone
I might not have been so impressed; but the contrast is so great, there is such a striking difference
between himself and Mr. Van Dusen, who, as
millionaires go, is apparently a very nice man, that
I was struck by it, and I certainly think Mr. Craik
suffers by the comparison.   He does not look one
in the eye frankly."

"His manner seemed perfect to me," said
Belle, "and he was the personification of gracefulness."

"Well, perhaps I am mistaken," said Nettie;
"but I never shall like him, of that I feel sure.
Why, what is the matter with the boat? we have
gained but very little distance since we started, and
see, we are drifting away from the shore fast."

"It must be the wind and tide," said Belle.
"Oh, dear, I am frightened.   Why *did* we come
so far away from Cup Island?   Tom will not like
it; but see, Nettie, the gentlemen see us.   They
evidently understand our predicament, and will
help us."

"Craik," said Van Dusen, after the girls had
rowed and drifted out of hearing, "those are two
fine-looking girls; about as pretty as I ever saw."

"By Jove, you are right," responded Craik.
"Where in the deuce did you meet them?"

"I never met Miss Knowles before; Miss Tillottson I saw at the Academy exhibition last fall.

I know her brother, Dr. Tillottson, very well. Miss Tillottson tells me they are camping on the little island, Cup Island I think they call it, near where we are anchored. She says her brother, the doctor, and a friend of his by the name of Stratton, are with them. I wonder if it is Stratton, the artist?"

Here an exclamation from Craik arrested his attention.

" They are not making any headway! See, they are drifting out with the strong tide!"

"So they are," said Van Dusen. "We must help them; we will row to their assistance."

This they proceeded at once to do. It did not take them long to reach the boat in which the girls were so unfortunately drifting, and taking their painter, they were soon slowly towing them in the proper direction. After fifteen or twenty minutes, however, of hard pulling, they had made but little progress, and were glad to see a sail-boat bearing down upon them from a distance. It contained Tom and Jack, who were returning from a fishing excursion, on which they had started in the early morning. As they drew near they recognized the girls by their dress and began to shout,—

" Hello, there," roared Jack. " Ship ahoy."

" Hello yourself," shouted Van Dusen, in a good-natured way. " Hurry up here and give us a lift, will you?"

"That is Van Dusen," said Tom. "I know his voice. Yes, they are towing the girls."

"Don't swing around too near them," said Jack; but the caution was unnecessary, for Tom rounded neatly up to Van Dusen's boat, and the whole party were soon on board of "The Queen," with their two boats in tow.

The story of their misfortunes was soon told by the girls while they were bowling along toward home under full canvas.

"I am greatly indebted to you, I am sure," said Tom, addressing Van Dusen, "for your kindness to these ladies."

"Oh, not at all, not at all," said Van Dusen, heartily; "don't mention it. You see I have been on a short foraging expedition, looking up some nice butter and eggs and spring chickens. I'm about to give a spread on Sunday on board of the 'Siren,' and I have been making sure of provisions enough up there at the old farm-house. By the way, why can't you all come over to-morrow and dine with us? Plain Sunday spread, you know; nothing very fancy or elaborate, but truly whole-some,—ha! ha! like the air here. The Van Twists are coming."

"Thank you," said Tom, "most happy;" and the others bowed their acceptance.

"Well, then, I'll tell Bolser"—Bolser was the cook—"to put on some extra plates; shall I hope to see your mother and aunt, doctor? Delighted to have them. Plenty of room."

" No, thank you," said Tom; "mother is hardly able yet to dine out, and, besides, you know, she must attend church, come what may."

" Yes, I know these old ladies," said Van Dusen; "and it's all right. Bless their dear souls, they keep us poor sinners straight!"

Arriving at Cup Island, Craik and Van Dusen, declining an invitation from Belle to walk up to the cottage, soon took their departure, Van Dusen as he stepped into his boat reminding them of their promise to meet the following day and stating that they would dine at two. The sun was high in the meridian, and the party were correspondingly high in spirits, as they ascended toward the cottage. Bid stood at the door in a clean white apron, her ruddy face beaming with a broad smile of welcome, which argued a good warm dinner, for which their adventures had well prepared them.

CHAPTER V.

An Interview with Mr. Beegum—The Incubator—A Letter from
Bob Evans—Fun in a Studio—Bid proves her Superior Tact—
A short Sketch of Aunt Deborah—Puritan Ancestry.

LIFE at Cup Island was by no means eventless
or monotonous. Our little party was always busy.
Sometimes they boarded "The Queen" for a fishing
excursion, lasting perhaps all day; or, the weather
being propitious, they would go for a long sail up
or down the coast, taking Bid along to cook for
them. On such occasions they would land where
the beach was sandy, build a fire, spread a cloth
upon the clean white sand, and enjoy repasts,
which Bid and the girls well knew how to produce. Sometimes they would visit one or another
of the many little villages scattered along the Connecticut shore, when they would take opportunity
to replenish their stock of provisions, or whatever
they needed in the way of supplies. They visited
Oldport often, soon becoming well acquainted with
the majority of its inhabitants. While they were
there on one occasion, Jack and the doctor, leaving the girls with Mrs. Tillottson, strolled up the
road in search of a man named Beegum, who they
had heard offered chickens for sale. Mr. Beegum,

they were informed, lived a mile or so northwest of the village, in a shanty just at the base of a high hill, which was pointed out to them at the Sandy cottage. Beegum, or Bigum, as his neighbors called him, was a widower and lived alone. He had never been what might be called a pecuniarily successful man, though there had been a time years before when he had inherited a considerable property. He was, however, in imagination, a man of wealth, and sanguine to an astonishing degree. He had sacrificed piece by piece and little by little all that he formerly possessed in futile attempts to carry out his plans. Reverses, however, had by no means shaken a firm faith in his ability to scheme and execute. "Trust Beegum for that," he would say when his method of effecting some impossibility was questioned. His married life had been happy, because the simple-minded, trusting little woman who shared his fortunes believed in him implicitly, and, although she saw his plans fail one by one, as regularly and surely as they were made, and his property slip away from him as a certain result, until he was absolutely penniless, she died at last, as she had lived, his foremost champion and the uncomplaining sharer of his defeats. Beegum was now about sixty years of age; but years never had brought him to that turning-point of careers, when an unfortunate but sanguine man begins to mistrust himself, or to suspect a weak spot in his own mental economy.

The young men found him at home. He responded in person to their summons. Short in stature almost to dwarfishness, with a head unusually large, a long, swaying body upon short, bowed legs, and a face which never seemed at rest, he was an individual who seemed to have jumped from boyhood to old age in a single night, taking with him the form, size, and, in some respects, the actions of extreme youthfulness.

" Is Mr. Beegum at home ?" said Tom, politely.

" Well, ruther, I should say," said the little man, smiling broadly. " That's me, gents; that's me. Come right in. I've been sorter spectin' ye fer a week or so. Of course, you're come to see my incubator ? I knew my last letter 'd fetch yer. I tell you what, it's a good thing, an' there's piles of spondulix in it."

He led them into a small front room, keeping up a running fire of words.

" Set down, set down, both on ye," said he, " an' I'll explain the workin' of the tarnal thing to ye. I tell you, gents, it hez taken brains to get that thing untangled. Yer see, too much heat kills 'em in the shell, and not enough heat kills 'em the same way by slow degrees, and——"

" I understand that you have chickens for sale ?"

said Tom, who had been striving to get in a word edgeways for some minutes.

"Yes; oh, yes; but, you see, I'm on'y workin' a bit of a model now of the incubator, and that on'y turns out from seven to a dozen a week. Why, sir, what do you think of two hundred an' fifty a day, or fifteen to seventeen hundred a week, makin', say, at a small calkerlation, ninety thousand two-legged chickens a year? Oh, I tell you, thar's money in it. I can feel it right now atween these ole fingers, but I must have money to git it under way; and it was reel good of yer to come to-day. I'll show yer my plans, an' then you'll be sure to want ter invest a few hundred dollars in such a good thing. As I said, I've been expectin' yer fer a week or so. When did you leave New York? That's a big place, isn't it? How they would stare and crowd around a windy in Broadway to see my incubator a-hatchin' out a chicken every five minutes! You better believe they would."

Here he chuckled to himself at the thought, and Tom, who now saw his golden opportunity, said, with an effort to keep a straight face,—

"Mr. Beegum, you are mistaken. We are perfect strangers to you, and stopping here near Oldport for the summer. We simply called upon you to purchase a few live chickens."

"An' ain't you neither on yer chicken-dealers?

An' ain't yer name Higgins ?" asked poor Beegum,
with a sort of groan.

"No, sir," said Tom. "We want to eat the
chickens."

"Well, bless my soul!" said Beegum, trying
nobly to cover up his disappointment. "I allowed yer was men from New York that I've
been a'writin' to about my incubator. But jest
let me show you my plans. Here yer see is the
heater, which I feed with this six-wicked coal-ile
burner; an' here I'm going to put a wire-nettin',
which tempers an' spreads the heat as it rises into
this cock-loft above."

"Yes," said Tom, firmly; "but we have ladies
waiting for us in the village, Mr. Beegum, and
will be compelled to leave you. Perhaps some
other time we will be able to listen to your plans
and look at your drawings. Now we must go,
unless you can sell us a dozen chickens right
away."

Beegum looked appealingly at Jack a moment,
but seeing the same look of determination upon
his face, and that they were fully decided to depart, he became suddenly as deeply interested in
the sale of his chickens as he had been in his
prospective incubator, and, after a little dickering,
sold them a dozen fine hens, which he promised
to deliver to Mr. Sandy in the morning, and, es-
corting them to the road, was profuse in his invi-

tations for them to come soon again and investigate his plans for a model incubator, which would
turn out over ninety thousand chickens a year
and surprise the world. There they left him ges-
ticulating at the gate as they walked back toward Oldport, restraining their hilarity until they
reached a convenient bend in the road. At the
post-office Jack received, among his letters, one
from his friend Robert Evans, in reply to his,
which we have read. It was written in a style
characteristic of Evans, and was so thoroughly
enjoyed by Jack that we will indulge the reader
with its contents :

" MY DEAR STRATTON,—Though it is insuffera-
bly hot in town, here I am just as I have been all
summer, sweltering in my little attic room, with
the mercury somewhere up in the nineties. Yesterday it dallied around ninety-four in the shady
shadow of my protecting roof-tree, and your humble
servant came within a peg or two of melting. To-
day it seems even warmer, so I am sitting négligé,
in my lofty apartment, with windows and doors
open wooing the breezes, which, by the way, don't
woo worth a cent. It is too hot to eat, drink, or
be merry; and as I breakfasted late, I don't expect a sign of an appetite to dawn upon my gastronomical horizon before night brings me a dimi-
nution of caloric. Thank your lucky stars, my

boy, that you are away from brick and mortar and this superlatively Hottentottish climate. I had the peaches sent as you directed and Scribbles' last agony. I would do more than this for admiration of the sweet face which you sent me. Allons! You are indeed a lucky dog to have Cup Island so quickly converted into a paradise. I have a strong mind to run down there and cut you out.

"Advice? Well, you are a ' chicken.' How can you expect a susceptible, inexperienced young flip like myself to send you advice?

" The boys at college, just before a race, used to say to me, ' Now, Bobbie, go in and win.' I would recommend the same advice to you, did I not know that you will do it any way. Phaint heart never won phair lady you know. I am digging away as usual, and have nearly finished the miser picture. Old Cripps, the model, poor old beggar, went sound asleep yesterday while I was getting in some neat work on his immaculate garments. Lawton came in, full of the old Harry as usual, and we decorated old Cripps while he innocently slumbered. We put a two-quart tin pail on his head, tied a clothes-line about his neck, attaching the free end to my sleeping dog, Bruno. Lawton then placed the skeleton gently in Cripps's lap, and dropped a few No. 8 shot into his boots. We then rolled the big mirror up in front of him, and watched his expression as we brought him to consciousness by stirring up Bruno to the tune of ' rats.'

"It would stagger a Shakespeare or a Hugo to describe the results of that experiment. Cripps certainly thought death held him an unwilling captive. I enclose a modified sketch of him as he appeared in death's embrace. Poor old Gripps. Lawton gave him a fiver for his fright, and he hobbled off on the No. 8 shot, thinking, probably, that fright had brought on a sudden case of bunions.

" Tell Tom I dropped around to his den yesterday, and Baker, M.D., was in good spirits and. seemed to be doing nicely. I shall be glad when you boys get back to Gotham. For heaven's sake, Jack, don't perpetrate any more rheumatic rhythm ; the weather is too warm, and, besides, it is a bad symptom. Tom will tell you that Bloomingdale has been reinforced for milder offences against sanity than that. No sane soul ever insisted that the heart of a pearl was blue.

" Take my advice, boy; stick to your brush, and let Milton and Longfellow sleep in peace.

" Now I'll shut the doors and take a snooze, for this temperature does not encourage wakefulness. Good-by, Jacob. Regards to Tom.

    " Yours, as ever,   Bob.

" P.S.—Be brave, old chap, be brave."

The following day, about noon, Sandy rowed over to Cup Island, carrying the dozen hens which he had tied in pairs by their feet.

"Whar d'ye want 'em, Dorkter?" said he to Tom, who with Jack stood on the landing.

Now it was a fact that neither Jack nor Tom had thought of this problem since the purchase of the birds; but Tom, not wishing to betray their improvidence, told Sandy, in an easy way, to let them loose upon the island, as they were neither web-footed nor fleet of wing.

"I reckon ye'll have a time ketchin' on 'em, Dorkter," said Sandy; "fur a hen is a lively critter when you want her for cookin' purposes." Saying which he released the hens by cutting the cords which secured them, and tossed them lightly upon the sand. The fowl, after looking about in a dazed sort of way, shaking out their rumpled plumage and stretching their cramped limbs, began to pick their way over the rocks in a dignified but uncertain manner toward a patch of ground which seemed to promise them a scanty breakfast.

"I brought ye over a peck o' corn an' a few pounds o' meal fur the chicks," said Sandy, laying them out upon the beach; "an' I reckon they'd fat up quicker ef they was cooped up. I allus fats mine in the dark." With which good advice he rowed away toward Oldport, with that easy but effective swing of the oars which is common to boatmen.

"Let us have broiled chicken for dinner to-morrow," said Tom to Jack and the girls, who with Bid had gathered at the pier to witness the landing of the pilgrims.

"Shure, an' ye'll be afther catchin' a coople o' 'em now thin, an' choppin' the heads off av the poor dears," said Bid, who was also standing upon the pier.

This was a contingency which now occurred to the young men for the first time and with sinking hearts. But they had handled wild duck when alive and wounded, and they were not to be put out by such a little thing as the slaughter of a hen, so Jack said, cheerfully,—

"All right, Bid," and proceeded at once to carry out her suggestion. The hens, however, were unusually shy, for when Jack approached they ambled off away from him uttering notes of alarm.

"I will head them off," said Tom, suiting the action to the word; but the birds scattered indiscriminately about as soon as they perceived themselves between two enemies, wildly half flew and ran in all directions, filling the air with their cacklings, and showing by their tactics that they were well up in warfare of this nature. Jack and Tom, however, were not to be outgeneralled in this way;

so, after a short consultation, during which there
was a decided expression of interest visible upon
the faces of the female witnesses, they each singled
out a victim and started confidently in hot pursuit.
Over rocks and under bushes they went, sometimes
so exasperatingly near the objects of their chase
that they would stretch forth an expectant hand,
when, alas! in a trice and by an artful dodge, the
hens would put rods of distance between them.
Finally, the hens one after another flew up into the
neighboring trees, and the young men were obliged
to give up the chase and acknowledge themselves
defeated.

"Never mind," said Belle, as they all returned
to the cottage, "we can easily do without the
broiled chickens."

There was, however, a mischievous look in her
eyes as she glanced toward Nettie, and the young
men noticed that the same mysterious expression
pervaded the faces of Nettie and Bid. Jack, who
felt desperate, sat for a little while in a brown
study and soon afterward was seen taking down
his gun.

"What are you going to do?" said Tom.

"I think I will go gunning," said Jack, with a
determined look; "and if I do not have pretty
good luck, I'm mistaken."

"Oh, Mr. Stratton, *please* do not shoot the poor,
dear chickens," said Belle, pleadingly.

"Rather tame sport for a hunter of reputation," said Tom, laughing uneasily.

"Well, it would be rather a barbarous way to obtain a brace of domestic fowl," said Jack, at the same time carefully putting up his gun.

"Shure, Misther Torm," said Bid, "wud yes give me a bit o' the male, an' oi wud be afther bringing yes a coople o' thim fowls in a jiffy."

Tom gave her the meal-bag, and soon Bid was hurrying over the ground in the direction of the hens, who were now peacefully scratching for a living at a distance.

"Chook! chook! chook!" said Bid, walking slower as she neared them. The hens looked up, but did not appear frightened at sight of a female. Bid rattled the spoon upon the tin pan in which she had mixed the meal into a sort of hasty-pudding with hot water. The hens appeared to know that breakfast was ready, and did not offer to run. Bid approached them now very slowly, stirring the meal and talking soothingly to the hens. When quite near them she dexterously threw upon the ground a little of the moist meal. There was an immediate scramble among the fowl to see who would get the first bite, during which Bid quietly squatted upon the ground, at the same time throwing a little more of the meal quite near to her. The hens approached fearlessly; in fact, they rushed directly at the meal. Then Bid quietly held the spoon with some meal in it so that by craning out their necks they could reach it. After the first mouthful or two they crowded around the spoon, eating voraciously. Two or three of the hens were more eager than the others, or more fearless, and as Bid placed the pan down upon the ground close beside her they immediately pounced upon it, their example being soon followed by nearly the whole flock. This gave Bid her well-earned opportunity, and quickly seizing two fat hens by their legs, she arose and bore them, squawking and flapping their wings, triumphantly to the cottage.

"Sure, an' 'tis aisy 'nuff, wud ye be gintle wid 'em," she said, nonchalantly, in reply to their congratulations; and a few moments later she was sitting upon a rock at the rear of the cottage industriously denuding the hens of their feathers, while Nettie and Belle audibly discussed the superiority of woman in an emergency where great tact and discretion were essential, much to the discomfiture or, perhaps we should say, to the entertainment of Jack and the doctor.

Meantime, Mrs. Tillottson's condition was rapidly improving at the Sandy cottage. Her life there, although not eventless, was rather a lonesome one. Her sister's company was not satisfying to her. They were so unlike in many respects. Early in life circumstances had drifted them away from each other. Deborah Tremane never in any way resembled her sweet sister Mary; and now, when the years had wrought so many changes and fate had again brought them together, it was not strange that the loving social ties of sisterhood had weakened by disuse.

Deborah had never married. The reasons for this were obvious; always provided with those comforts which make home pleasant, and leading a life without a thought of the future, she had naturally not entertained notions of matrimony. Brought up in the country, where she saw little of society, she interested herself mostly with those things which floated under her direct observation. In many respects she was an excellent house-keeper. Warm-hearted, in a spontaneous sense, she never was at a loss either for words or action. Unlike Mary, her sister, she was very plain in appearance and rather simple in mind, which latter deformity had never stimulated her to a thorough cultivation of her naturally limited mental possibilities.

While Mary was at finishing school, receiving the polish which was to aid her through life, Deborah was content to help their good mother at housekeeping, or to ride galloping about the country on their dun-colored cob, gathering bits of news or gossiping with the neighbors. Thus it happened that Deborah grew up into woman-

hood a sort of good-natured ignoramus, but at
the same time as facile of tongue as it is possible
to conceive.   Perhaps this extreme loquacious-
ness had saved her from matrimonial fetters; certain it is that, although young men showed a decided preference for her good mother's apples
and cider, and though they always appeared glad
of Deborah's society, there never was one glad
enough to ask her for a life-interest in it.

So when her sister Mary married and left the
homestead, Deborah stayed on, the same chatty,
thoughtless creature, until one day her mother
died and left her alone a comparatively old woman
and without home-ties.

After the funeral, her sister Mary had lovingly
put her arms about her, and offered to share her
home.   So the old house was closed, and Deborah
Tremane became a permanent member of the Tillottson family.   She was short of stature, of
lightish complexion, and possessed a face which,
although by no means handsome, marked her as
a woman of good motive and kindly disposition.

"Sister Mary," she said one day to Mrs. Tillottson, after the girls had made their customary visit,
" don't you think we'd both on us feel a sight
easier if we was with Belle and the rest on Cup
Island?   I mean if we was there all the time;
not but what it is nice here, an' I'm sure we're
both growing strong and fat, for Mrs. Sandy is an

awful nice cook, an' knows a thing or two 'bout housekeeping; but if we was on the island we would not be so much alone as we are here, an' we could have an eye out for the comfort of those young folks. Bid is a good girl enough, but, law sakes, what does she know about them youngsters ?"

"Well, I don't know, Deborah," said Mrs. Tillottson; "I hardly think there would be room for so many in that little cottage. However, we will go over and investigate some day, and if they all think it is feasible we will try it."

"Yes, that's it," said Deborah; "we will go over an' see; an' if it is possible to squeeze us in there, I think we will feel easier an' more sociable-like than we do here; although I've nothing to say agin Mrs. Sandy, who is a mighty clever, home-like sort of a body. She knows I want to go over to the island to live, for I told her. Here she comes now. Now, Mrs. Sandy, we was just talkin' it over 'bout goin' over to Cup Island to live with the young folks. Of course you know, as I was tellin' you afore, that we ain't dissatisfied here at all, only I was jest a-tellin' my sister it would be more like home to be with the children ; an' you know them gals haven't any one to look after them but two boys an' Bid, who knows more 'bout nursin' than she does about the wants of two young ladies."

"Well, if you think you'd be comfortable-like over there," said Mrs. Sandy, "I'm sure I should go if I was you, though goodness knows I like well 'nough to have you stay here as long as you feel like it. I was a-tellin' Sam to-day that I never had city folks here before who made so little trouble; for generally when they come it's all fuss an' feathers."

"Well, if we *is* city folks," said Deborah, with a clear accent and a position a little more erect,— "if we *is* city folks, we know what's what, an' we don't want to put folks as ain't city folks to any trouble or bother that can be helped; do we, Mary?"

But Mary had quietly departed, as was her custom when such conversations were taking place.

It was somewhat of a trial to Mrs. Tillottson to have a rustic sister so constantly with her; but she was too heroic to put an end to it by separation, and, on the whole, she took an inward pleasure in the sacrifice of her feelings. Mrs. Tillottson was one of those thoughtful women who, although they possess a modicum of family pride, recognize the fact that few families when viewed through a long line of New England ancestry fail to develop instances here and there of the tape-measuring element, and although her own progenitors were, from her father, who was a man of the cloth, to the primeval ancestor who stepped off of the " Mayflower," all professional men, she was liberal enough in her feelings to concede an equality of excellence in others so long as they kept up the essential social requisites of morality and politeness. Indeed, it was prominently apparent that her sister Deborah Tremane possessed much more of what is called family pride than Mrs. Tillottson. Deborah never lost an opportunity to bring this subject clearly before an indulgent listener.

"As far as money goes," she would say, "I know our folks don't take the lead, though we always had a roof to cover our heads and everything that ordinary folks needs to make 'em comfortable; but when it comes to pedigree, we can hold up our heads as high as any of 'em, for from Michael Tremane, who first come over in the ' Mayflower,' to my dear father who was a preacher of the gospel, our men folks have all been leaders, doctors, lawyers, and sich. Sometime I will show you some of the letters which my great-grandfather, who was a surgin in the army under George Washington during the revolutionary war,—I say I will show you some of the letters he writ home to his wife, Melindy. They are the sweetest, nicest writ letters I ever read, an' writ in them heathen times, too; it is really wonderful."

CHAPTER VI.

A Letter from Rome—Adam Dexter's Grief—A Severe Shock—
Tom and Nettie become Metaphysical—Jack's Idea of Florence—Natural Physiognomists.

ADAM DEXTER, Nettie's uncle, sat in his cool
breakfast-room on the 25th of July, calmly looking
over his mail. One by one he read the letters
before him, pausing now and then to comment
upon them to himself. He had nearly finished
when he noticed one which bore a foreign stamp
and post-mark. Opening it with some curiosity,
he read as follows :

"ROME, ITALY, June —, 18—.

"MR. ADAM DEXTER :

"*My Dear Sir,*—Prepare yourself for most
startling news of your long-lost son. Painful as
the duty is, it devolves upon me to inform you of
his recent death. This duty is made doubly
painful and distressing to me from the fact that he
was my best, my dearest friend. He confided to
me just before his death the particulars of his
quarrel with you so many years ago, how he left
your home in a moment of passion and indignation never to return, and with tearful eyes he
poured this unfortunate story of his youth into my

ears. He said that the recollection of your last
unnatural words to him had often killed his renewed intention to return to your roof and ask
your forgiveness.

"Ah, sir, you could not have known the pure
gold in his heart when you so coldly and cruelly
drove him from you.

"His death was a sad and most unfortunate one.
I fear, I may say, he was murdered. It happened
in the following manner:

"Your son, known here as Dexter Rogers, was
attending a ball given by the Countess Finnotti.
He was a great favorite with the Countess, who is
one of our most cultivated and esteemed women.

"He was seldom absent from her receptions,
and was always willing and ready to aid her in
pleasing and entertaining her guests. It was at
one of these receptions that he received his death-
wound. It seems that one Antoinne De Lacey, a
man of very pleasing manners and great personal
attractions to ladies, was one of the invited guests.
I have since learned that this man is an adventurer
and a scoundrel; that he made his *entrée* into our
society by means of forged letters of introduction.
On this particular evening at the entertainment,
he, for some reason, appeared to become heated
with wine and to lose control of himself, offending
several ladies, and finally, grossly insulting the
Countess herself. Roger, who happened to be

standing near, remonstrated with him, attempting to lead him away. At this, De Lacey, becoming enraged, struck Roger, who, finding that he must defend himself, knocked the rascal down.

"Struggling to his feet again, however, De Lacey drew a pistol and fired, the shot taking effect in your son's breast.

"During the confusion which immediately ensued the villain escaped.

"It has since developed that the whole fracas was an imbroglio planned by several desperadoes to rob the apartments of the Countess. This was thoroughly done during the intense excitement which followed the shooting. At first we thought that your son was not seriously injured, he laughing at the wound, assuring his friends that it was trivial, and walking without assistance to his carriage; but there was difficulty in finding the bullet, which had found lodgment in the joint of his shoulder, and after a few days a serious fever set in, and Roger was delirious. He was even then not considered seriously wounded by his physicians; but his condition, week after week, became gradually worse, until, after two months of intense suffering, but heroic endurance, he died. His physicians disagreed as to the actual cause of his death, one stating his opinion that it was blood-poisoning, and the other two maintaining that he had contracted a malignant fever.

"We were partners in the same banking-business ; and I am glad to say that he has been very fortunate in all of his business ventures. You are, of course, aware that the firm of Wigand & Rogers is, and has been for some years, the leading banking-house in Italy. Your son has, by prudence, good judgment, and judicious management, accumulated great wealth. This fortune, which will probably amount to half a million in your money, he has left, unconditionally, by will, to his cousin, Miss Knowles, of whose welfare and movements, as well as your own, he has kept himself fully informed during his residence in Italy. I enclose a letter written by him to his cousin, informing her of his desire to make her his heir. He informed me that you were financially independent, and would be pleased that your niece should be sole heir to his valuable estate. I enclose a photograph of the deceased, my dear sir, and the address of his attorney here, with whom you can immediately communicate with reference to prompt settlement. The remains of my beloved friend I have had carefully embalmed, and they await your direction. I also enclose a likeness of the scoundrel, De Lacey, who was probably the cause of your son's unfortunate and early death, thinking that possibly he may have taken flight to America, and that it may lead to his detection and capture. He may easily be identified by a peculiar deformity of the little finger of his right hand, which he is unable to close or bend,—that is, when he closes his right hand this one finger remains extended, and is therefore conspicuous. I am informed by the police that in England he was known as 'James Bolan,' or 'Gentleman Jim;' that he is by no means a common scoundrel, but can deceive the most cultured people by his grace of manner, gentlemanly bearing, and wily tongue.

"Now, my dear sir, let me again assure you that you have my heartfelt sympathy, and kindest hopes that you may be able to bear this terrible blow with courage.

"Most respectfully yours,

.   "Moses Wigand."

Can you imagine, dear reader, the intensity of suffering and shame which this letter brought to Adam Dexter? In a moment of passion he had denounced his youthful son as unworthy of him; and with a fierce curse had sent him from his presence, never, alas! to see him again alive. The offence of the boy was a severe one, to be sure, for he had spoken falsely; but the punishment—ah—that was what was now racking the father's long-suffering heart as he pictured his only son dying in a foreign land, and then realized what might have been. He sat for an hour with his head

upon the table weeping like a child. The servants came in and passed out again respectfully,
not wishing or daring to disturb such grief. He
had long since repented his treatment of his boy
Roger; in fact, before he had been absent two
days he had scoured the immediate country for
him, afterward advertising far and wide, and finally
he had sought him himself over the world. But
Roger for several years was at sea and never
knew of his father's desire to forgive and be for-
given.

Nettie had in some measure compensated for
Roger's absence, taking the boy's place in the
father's affections; and he had at last persuaded
himself that Roger was dead and therefore out
of trouble. Nettie, however, knew that on every
anniversary of Roger's birth his father spent the
entire day in his room, and such was the nature
of his grief that for several days after these annual
events he was, although tender and gentle with
her, absent-minded, and irritable with strangers
and the servants. The same instinctive tenacity,
which kept the son away, gnawed at the heart of
the father in the shape of the painful consciousness
that he had been terribly unjust.

With Nettie it was different. At first she seemed
unconsolable, and her sorrow, though paroxysmal,
was acute; but as the months and years rolled by
and the memories of Roger were always pleasant,

she grew to look upon him almost as a pleasing
creation of the imagination, seldom thinking of
him as a reality. Thus does time discriminate.
With the guilty it creates remorse and uncouth
images which fester in the recollection; while to
the innocent it stretches forth a caressing hand,
the soft strokes of which smooth out the wrinkles
of care and mellow all that is grievous to
memory.

At last one of the maids, becoming alarmed and
a little impatient at Mr. Dexter's long silence,
approached him and said in a respectful manner,—

"Shall I remove the things, sir?"

Receiving no response, she repeated the inquiry
in a louder voice; still getting no reply, she became frightened and called the other servants,
who soon discovered that their employer was perfectly helpless. They removed him gently to his
room and bed, immediately summoning the family
physician, who at once pronounced the trouble to
be a severe shock of paralysis. For several days
he lay almost lifeless, but breathing regularly,
otherwise showing no power; at last, however,
after much care and attention from his physician
he seemed able to slightly move his arms and
hands. This was a joyful moment to him, as he
was very desirous to impart some information to
his physician, and was unable to utter a word of
speech. At the end of a week he indicated by

signs that he wanted writing-materials, and when these were given him he managed with much difficulty and in a cramped hand to write that he did not wish his condition made known to his niece until later in the season, as he did not desire to mar the enjoyment of her visit with her friends. He said that he hoped and expected to recover enough to lessen the shock, which the knowledge of his affliction would give her. Thus it happened that Nettie did not receive either news of her uncle's illness, of Roger's death, or of her own good fortune in becoming his heir, until several weeks afterward. She entered into all of the sports at Cup Island, and gave herself wholly to the festivities of the hour.

The day following the adventure upon the beach was Sunday. It was a perfect day, and during the long morning hours the party of four sat in the summer-house or lounged about the island. Belle had an interesting book, which she persuaded Jack to read aloud to her, while Nettie and Tom gathered shells along the shore, chatting intelligently about the many things which are sure to find their way to the surface of such minds as theirs.

" How strange," said Nettie; " how very strange is the life of a fish. Suppose, for instance, that I were a fish and had the same power of thought which I now possess; I would behold with amaze-

ment the creatures who could live out of water.
I would look upon them as ethereal beings, or as
I should recognize angels or ghosts, should they
appear to me now.   I think I would not, were I
a fish, envy such beings their existence who could
live and breathe out of water.   Perhaps, in my
estimation, I would place them upon a lower plane
than my own, since they were incapable of doing
as I did."

"If you were a fish," said Tom, laughing, "I
am certain that I would turn fisherman, and would
never be contented until I had used every available means known to fishermen, by hook or by
crook, to catch you."

"You overlook an important feature of my supposition," said Nettie, with a bland smile, "which
was, that in addition to being a fish I should have
the same power of thought which I now possess."

"Granted," said the doctor, gayly ; "but my bait
would be the bait of human kindness; my line
and hook would simulate other charming qualities,
which would surely catch the hungry eye of such
a fish."

"After which I should be a pitiful, one-eyed
fish," laughed Nettie.   "Oh, that would be cruel.
But, seriously, if *you* were a fish, and at the same
time had the intelligence which is now your right,
what think you would be your impressions of the
aerial world of living creatures ?"

"That depends," said Tom, seriously, and with great deliberation, "upon what creatures or creature passed before my piscatorial vision. Now, if I saw you, for instance——"

"No, no," said Nettie, interrupting him a little impatiently; "answer me seriously. You know I do not fish for compliments, and it is almost cruel for you to so misconstrue the object of my question."

Tom sobered down instantly, and, in an earnest tone and a manner worthy of a true philosopher, said,—

"If I were what you supposed,—which of course would be impossible,—I should lose my faith in a kind Creator. I would be a man in desire, affections, intelligence, ambition,—all of those mental and moral qualities which men possess,—yet confined, by the decree of my Creator, within the disgraceful possibilities of a fish. I would see human beings doing what I desired to do, acting as I desired to act, living as I desired to live, yet would be but a fish with a fish's limited power. I should curse myself and try to die. But, by the kind dispensation of divine Providence, such cruelties are not permitted. Animals always possess intelligence in proportionate harmony with the tenor of their existence; were it otherwise, chaos would usurp the place of order or acting natural laws.

"An oyster is as happy in oysterdom as a

Christian in Christendom, because he realizes
only those things which regulate his existence
as an oyster. This intelligent faculty in animals
and plants is called instinct, and differs from that
of man by virtue of the fact that man possesses
free-will; and to admit this latter assertion em-
phatically presupposes a future life for man. So
now, you see, Miss Knowles, you have succeeded
in getting me, in spite of myself, into deep water
by your hint that I might be a fish."

"I am pleased with your reply," said Nettie,
repentantly; "for you have touched upon a subject
which has long deeply interested me, and which I,
too, acknowledge is beyond my depth."

"Better become a fish, like myself," said Tom,
quickly. "We fish like deep water."

"No, thank you," replied Nettie; "not with
human intelligence. It seems to me we have
enough trouble as human beings without adding
the dreadful condition which you have just pictured."

"But," continued Tom, "we are so constituted,
by affection and intelligence, that we can overcome trouble; the fish has no trouble, because he
has no capacity to suffer."

"Are not the small fish in danger of being de-
voured by the large?" she asked.

"Yes," said Tom, thoughtfully; "but can they
not seek the shallow water for protection? Their

limited brain-power prevents their brooding over trouble. The pickerel or the trout is so ravenous by nature that he will snap at new bait while the wound of a hook is fresh, or perhaps the hook itself is hanging in his jaw. They hardly reason from cause to effect; some animals seem to possess this power, though even they are unable to syllogize. A crow will avoid a man who carries a gun, but if the man disguises himself as a female, the crow, although still shy, will permit much nearer approach, even though the gun is still in sight. A fox will avoid one kind of trap to step cautiously into another with which he is not so familiar.

"I once knew of a horse, owned by a pious farmer, who had been in the habit of taking the family to church on Sunday for many years. The road to the church was a branch of the main road to the village. On week-days the horse would never voluntarily go down the church-road; but on a Sabbath, without the slightest hint from the reins or his master, he would turn dutifully down the road which led to church. Did he know by the tolling of the church-bell that his duty led him in that direction on Sunday?

"Most probably, because on one week-day as his master was driving him to the village the bell was ringing, and the old horse quietly turned down the road to church, as a matter of course.

Until this last incident occurred the simple people to whom he belonged gave the horse credit for possessing an intelligence to which he was not fairly entitled. They thought he could distinguish between a Sabbath- and a week-day by counting the days.

"Lower animals do not reason intelligently, but merely exercise that modicum of instinct which their simple lives demand; hence their sufferings are by no means poignant.

"Nature—animal (excepting man), vegetable, and mineral—resembles a huge machine. It has many parts, but each part has its specific duty to perform, and would be useless elsewhere. A bird would make a sorry fish; a serpent would make a despicable flower. Man has power over all the fish of the sea, fowl of the air, and over every living thing that moves, because he is made in the image and likeness of God; but man, unlike these animate things of nature, has free-will; thus is the image and likeness made more perfect. If he exercises this power of free-determination rightly, care, suffering, trouble, anxiety are all impossible to him. Of course, this would be the picture of a perfect man (Adam before the fall). But men are not perfect; they have perverted the image and likeness to God, and therefore have suffering and troubles. A delicate prismatic glass globe is a beautiful thing, and has its uses; but if we use it for a foot-ball it loses its usefulness at the first kick. It is in a similar way that men pervert their freedom. Free-will is God-likeness; it is the one sublime faculty which makes man noble; but it must be used like the glass globe, —properly; pervert it, and men, who otherwise would be angels, become devils.

"In this simple truth lies the secret of life."

"Oh, thanks; many, many thanks, Dr. Tillott-son," said Nettie, enthusiastically, her beautiful eyes radiant with pleasure and gratitude. "The problem of living is clearer to me now than it ever has been. I infer from what you have stated that the most perfect people simply obey God's laws, which are found in the decalogue, and that, as none obey to the letter, troubles must come to us all."

"Yes," said Tom, "in the abstract, you are correct. Man is a little world, a microcosm; all things in nature have in him their correspondence; hence, as nature fails when natural laws are violated, so man fails when he violates spiritual laws or the laws of God. This is sin; nothing more or less. Sin is not an entity; it is a nonentity. It is the violation of moral laws, or rather the failure to observe them."

"These ideas are beautiful," said Nettie; "they are poetic."

"Yes," said the doctor, "they emanated from

the greatest poet and philosopher that the world
has ever produced."

" Can you forgive me for thinking you frivolous
a few moments ago ?" said Nettie, casting a timid
glance of entreaty, not unmixed with favor, at
Tom. " I can hardly forgive myself."

Tom laughed aloud. " Indeed, you have my
full pardon," said he, " provided you will fulfil one
or the other of two conditions."

" Name them," said Nettie, bravely.

" Either release me at once from imprisonment
as a fish, or immediately transform yourself into
one of the same species. You notice my forgiveness is conditional."

" Well, since you have so fairly earned your
freedom, I release you at once," replied Nettie,
laughing and blushing, as only pure natures are
wont to blush.

" Thank fortune I am a man again," said the
doctor, pretending to stretch himself; " now let us
talk of worldly matters."

" I am afraid," said Nettie, " if I wish you to
talk as I like, in the future I shall be obliged to
resort to the transformation act. Metamorphosis
seems to work like a charm in opening the flood-
gates of your speech."

It was by such familiar interchanges of wit and
thought that Nettie and Tom rubbed off the shy-
ness of new acquaintance and became stanch

friends who could chat together after the manner of the most congenial natures.

Meanwhile Jack, having tired of reading aloud, had been entertaining Belle by relating some of his experiences in Italy, and his struggles as a rising young artist.

" Life in Florence," Jack was saying, as the other two strolled up to where they were sitting, " is not calculated to infuse much ambition into a man unless his soul is devoted to art. It has a climate which begets lassitude and promotes sentiment. It is pre-eminently a city of associations and traditions. The home of Dante, of Galileo, and other equally famous men, it is, of course, calculated to inspire one with more or less reverence, and it is notably a city of art. Beautiful statuary abounds everywhere, and one is constantly looking at some production by which his tastes are unconsciously elevated; but the people, with their conceit and eccentricities, weary one. It is refreshing to meet an American. After all, there is no place like home."

" Except Cup Island," said Nettie, gayly.

" And that is a sort of temporary home; at any rate, we must consider it so," said Tom, pleasantly; " but it is about time we prepared to depart. It is now after one, and Van Dusen expects us on the ' Siren' by two o'clock."

They all acted readily upon Tom's suggestion,

and repaired to the cottage, appearing before many minutes ready for the short row to the yacht. While they were in the boat Jack said, in a sort of meditative way, "I am haunted by the face of that man Craik."

"A very handsome face, I am sure," said Belle, roguishly; but Jack, without seeming to heed her remark, continued,—

"I have certainly seen his features somewhere before, but where, puzzles me greatly. Of one thing I am positive; the impression that they make upon me is unfavorable. Where could it have been? I shall puzzle it out some time, I am sure."

"Perhaps," said Belle, "it was in a dream, and dreams go by contraries, you know."

"No," Jack replied; "I seldom dream; and when I do, it makes no impression upon my memory. I have surely met this man somewhere, for, besides a natural love of physiognomy, I have a good recollection for faces, and his face I remember well;" saying which he took from his pocket a small sketch-book, and, tearing from it a leaf, quickly sketched a likeness of Craik's face, surmounted by the broad-brimmed Panama hat. They all admitted that the resemblance to the original was very striking. Jack had proved himself a natural physiognomist by giving the picture an exaggerated character. He had portrayed the features excellently, and it was unmistakably the representation of a very handsome man; but it was so ingeniously drawn that the true character of the individual was apparent. It was a well-executed caricature, but would instantly be pronounced a remarkable likeness.

Carlyle once said, "Often I have found a portrait superior in real instruction to half a dozen written biographies, as biographies are written; or, rather let me say, I have found that the portrait was a small lighted *candle*, by which the biographies could for the first time be *read* and some human interpretation be made of them." Carlyle's descriptions of the faces, of the characters in his histories and books, are so lucid, so vivid, that one can almost feel their living presence. Here, for instance, is his description, or word-sketch, of Daniel Webster,—

"As a logic-fencer, or parliamentary Hercules, one would incline to back him at first sight against all the extant world. The tanned complexion, that amorphous crag-like face, the dull black eyes, under their precipice of brows, like dull anthracite furnaces, needed only to be blown; the mastiff-mouth, accurately closed; I have not traced as much of silent *Berserker* rage that I remember of in any other man."

What Carlyle so ably described in words, Jack could portray with his pencil and brush; and here in this picture, which he had made from his memory of Craik, was plainly shown the face of a wicked, cruel, calculating man. There was the dishonest droop of the eyelid over the cunning corner of the dark, unloving eye, overwrought perhaps in the drawing, but true enough to life; there was the mouth, thin of lips, and lacking the graceful curves which indicate an affectionate nature; there were the tell-tale lines of dissipation and avarice, all exaggerated, but indicating a nature which in the picture impressed them all unfavorably.

CHAPTER VII.

Dinner on the " Siren"—Communion of Soul—Tom as an Oracle —Dry Food for Craik—The Minister and the Professor—Visions of a Sea-Serpent—Prefiguration—No Proof of Continuous Evolution—Tom gives up a Luxury—A Villain at Large —Newspapers.

THE dinner on board of the "Siren" was a success. Van Dusen was a man who delighted in nothing more than in entertaining. Cordial, fond of anecdote, a fair judge of human nature, he made an excellent host, exhaling such an atmosphere of contentment and good humor that his guests at once felt comfortable and welcome. At his right hand sat Major and Mrs. Van Twist, and farther on Mr. Craik, Miss Van Twist, and Professor Romney; on his left, in respective order, were Belle, Jack, Nettie, Tom, and the parson, Mr. Kendall, who sat at the other end of the table, *vis-à-vis* to the host.

Professor Romney, who counted one of the yachting party, was a tall, military-looking individual, the lines of whose face and figure were strangers to roundness,—in fact, the only roundness about him seemed concentrated in his eyeglasses, which sat archly upon his Greco-American nose, and were calculated to surprise one into the belief that they were the eyes of a fierce monster glaring out of the dark recesses behind them. Professor Romney proved, however, during the dinner, that, although spare in person, he was by no means destitute of ideas or information. The customary courtesy to the presence of a man of the cloth having been said in the shape of grace, and the first urgent desires of appetite satisfied, the excellently-cooked food seemed gradually to lubricate the tongues of all present, and a general hum of conversation attested to their satisfaction and contentment.

Mr. Craik entertained Miss Van Twist with a description of Spanish hotel-life, occasionally glancing over at Belle, as if for approval. Jack

i

also gave some of his impressions upon the same
subject, while Mr. Van Dusen, after skilfully putting in a word here and there to encourage a general communion of soul, devoted himself to the
martyrdom of listening to Mrs. Van Twist's experiences as a financier,—a topic, by the way, of
which she never tired, especially when the listener
was as polite a millionaire as her host. Tom, who
was industriously dissecting a tempting cut of
broiled blue-fish, roguishly asked Nettie, in an
undertone, if she was sure she could enjoy the
idea of eating fish since, in her imagination, she
had so recently transformed him into one.

"It would be a pity to devour so much intelligence," Nettie replied, despairingly, "even in imagination." Here she laid down her fork. "But
I am neither going to allow you to tease me, nor
do I intend to get angry with you after your
learned discourse of this morning; so, on the
whole, I think I will finish my fish," taking up
her fork again and putting it to good use.

"Then I die happy," said Tom. "Shakespeare,
I think, has said, 'Dainty bits make rich the ribs,
but bankrupt quite the wits.' It is evident that
the immortal bard was mistaken. What a bless-
ing it is to eat and really enjoy eating."

"Yes," said Nettie. "I have read that Cleo-
patra held sway over Cæsar as much by her excellent suppers as by her personal charms."

"Yes, indeed," said Tom, amused; "and I believe it is authentic history that one of England's kings—Harry the Eighth, may be—expressed his gratitude to a man who discovered a new dish, of which he became very fond, by presenting him with an estate. Those were days when people had appreciative appetites, and it seems to me I can understand this better since I came to Cup Island."

"And I," said Nettie, laughing,—"I am actually astonished at myself, I eat so much; but, let me ask you, are you serious when you use the term 'authentic history'?"

"It was a slip of the tongue," said Tom, laughing. "I used it because I have seen it somewhere in print. Of course, it is a contradiction of terms; but, speaking of gratitude for gastronomic favors, does it not strike you that the divorce-list would amazingly decrease if married women would devote themselves a little more assiduously to cookery?"

"Yes," said Nettie, "I know it; and I always said that when I married I should make a study of my husband's epicureanism, and so win untold favors and limitless regard through that important channel."

"And do you really believe that the highway to a man's heart is through his stomach?" asked Tom, semi-seriously.

"Never mind what I believe," said Nettie, shocked at the doctor's plain language and not desiring to give him any more satisfaction.

Mr. Kendall, the clergyman, who by the way possessed a loud voice which he seldom seemed to think it necessary or wise to modulate, had been discussing the subject of card-playing with the professor. The clergyman held that the custom was bad for children on account of the evil associations connected with it.

"I tell you, sir," said he, in his vociferous way, arresting for a moment the attention of all present, his metallic voice sounding a double echo from the empty wine-glasses near him,—"I tell you, sir, that more mischief has been accomplished in the way of bringing young people into bad company through the medium of cards, or card-playing, than in almost any other way. It is not so much the actual playing of cards which is so objectionable, but it is what the habit leads to,—its results. I never play myself, from principle; but, of course, I do not seriously object to seeing our good friend Van Dusen and his friends enjoy themselves here occasionally with cards; they know their own strength. The crying evil is in allowing children to acquire the habit."

Here he seemed to stop, either because he had just missed a forkful of macaroni on its way to his mouth or because he had abruptly reached the end of his logical lane, and Tom modestly ventured to lift his voice.

"My parents," said he, gently, "always allowed me to play at cards. I built card-houses when a baby. My father played, my mother played, and their friends often dropped in of an evening for a social game of whist. Cards to me have the dearest associations. A friend of mine, however, was reared differently; he was taught that cards were a crying evil; whenever he ventured to import a pack into the family they were immediately confiscated and consumed. The result was that he played cards in his father's barn on the sly. I played openly in my father's house. Boswell once asked Johnson if he did not consider a certain piece of statuary indecent. 'No, sir,' said the doctor; 'but your remark is.' I know little about gambling, as to how or where it is carried on. How can cards with me have had an evil influence? I think they never had. It seems to me it is the motive in the individual which makes a habit or an action evil or good."

"Ah, yes," said Mr. Kendall, not noticing that a long string of macaroni had lodged in his beard, where it was making frantic swinging efforts to escape, "that is it exactly; it is the motive, sir; but a child has no definite motive; he should be under the surveillance or constant guidance of his parents, who should warn him of the breakers ahead, help him over them, and shield him from evils."

"True," said Tom, becoming at last quite interested in the discussion and striving to ignore the macaroni, which he knew by instinct that Belle and Nettie were exchanging glances about, "when there *are* breakers ahead; but is it wise, nay, is it just, to teach a child that whist, for instance, is an evil and card-playing pernicious, when other games equally innocent are allowable and enjoyed?   Would not the inconsistency of such a statement arouse the child's curiosity and indignation, and would there not be danger of his seeking the barn or privacy to do his playing? Rather than to so unjustly deceive a child of mine, I would prefer to take him when he is old enough into some gambling den, where I could teach him to appreciate its horrors. I would show him with a shudder the haggard, careworn faces of the players as they stake their last dollar, lose it, and rise with agonized faces to leave the room and return to a comfortless home ; or I would explain to him the avaricious grin of selfish delight which distorts the visages of those who win. He should understand how transparent is the delight of such and how heart-rending the despair of their victims. I think there are few children, if any, who, if clearly instructed about the horrors of evil-doing, would fail to profit by it, at least at some period of their lives. Such a course, however, necessitates a happy home and perfect behavior in the instructor."

"Did you ever mould in clay, sir?" asked the professor of Tom.

"No; I never tried it," Tom replied, smiling, and the clergyman shook his head also in the negative, causing the restless macaroni to form a figure suggestive of the much-observed sea-serpent.

"Well, it is a most delightful occupation," continued the professor, reflecting the pleasant expression of Tom's face and that of Belle and Nettie, who were both closely observing the antics of the sea-serpent.

"It is astonishing what marked facial changes one can produce with a very slight alteration in the clay. Suppose you were modelling the head of a man, for instance, you produce features which as they grow are pleasing, the eyes and mouth smile, and as you progress your heart joins your hands in your work, you actually begin to admire the muddy head before you. It shows traits of character which you did not dream that you could produce. You are drawn into a sort of friendly intercourse with it, as with some interesting new-made friend.

"Now, if your courage be equal to the experiment, take your moulding-stick and roughly press it into the corners of the eyes and mouth, just four quick pressures made at random, and behold, your good-natured friend has flown; while in his stead is a countenance which looks capable of murder, or worse yet, a four hours' harangue in the House on the tariff. Now children, it seems to me, are modelled very much like clay; if one is careful with every stroke of the instrument he will obtain a child-image which will delight the eye; but if he shuts his eyes, allows the stick to make random ravages, it will assume some hideous shape.

" I never see a very bad child but I think that its guardians must have moulded carelessly. There may be exceptions; if so, I hope they prove the rule, but I am convinced that good example is more effective than good precept. Both are indispensable to proper home training."

This was a long speech for the professor, and it was evident to the girls that he had not discovered the sea-serpent.

" Of course you do not except the importance of Sunday-school," said Mr. Kendall; the sea-serpent meantime diving into the very depths of his black beard and reappearing on its lower border.

" With all due deference, no," said the professor, not referring to the sea-serpent; " and yet, let me ask you what the impressions made upon a child's mind by the constant changes of doctrine must lead to ? If not to skepticism, or at least to agnosticism, or indifference, what then ?"

Jack, who had hitherto been fiercely struggling to overcome a great commotion among his risibilities, for his eyes had for some time been divided between the antics of the sea-serpent and the faces of the girls, now pricked up his ears. He was inclined to favor agnosticism, and felt that the conversation was about to become interesting. The Van Twists had a sleepy look, particularly the major, who nodded over his wine; Mr. Craik looked bored, while Mr. Van Dusen, who had seen the sea-serpent, wore a most indulgent expression.

Tom saw Jack's interest, and noticed a look of great concern upon the faces of Nettie and Belle, who had heard the professor's last remark. True, women never like to hear religion attacked. They are its natural champions, having an instinctive feeling that it is their main anchorage. They feel as though it was the keystone in life's frail arch. They know intuitively that, should this prop be taken away, the two sides which complete the arch—love and intelligence, or more explicitly, goodness and truth—would fall and meet destruction. With such a fall they realize that complete annihilation to matrimony and home would surely follow. They know, *de profundis*, without thought, that beneath this arch, beneath life's fragile bridge, over which they now so confidently tread, flows the murky, turgid river of destruction, reeking

with polygamy, free-love, blasphemy, and perdi-
tion. They know full well, as their gaze meets
this treacherous flood below, what the overthrow
of this bridge would involve; their dear faces
blanch at the thought, and their pure hearts grow
faint within them.

The professor was one of those men who are
constantly meddling with the foundations of
things. He was very much like the Irishman
whose duty it was to saw off a limb from one of
New Haven's stately elms. He straddled the
limb facing the trunk and deliberately sawed himself into heaven, for being upon the branch which
fell, he fell with it.

The clergyman not replying immediately, Tom,
who had now forgotten the sea-serpent, said,—

"Why should a change of doctrines appear in-
consistent when fundamental truths remain unchanged? I was taught at Sunday-school that
there was a God, and that He made all things. I
have always believed it."

"Were you taught that there were three Gods
and yet one?" asked the professor, quickly.

"Yes," replied Tom; "and the inconsistency of
the statement troubled me greatly."

"We must have faith to believe," said Mr. Kendall; "faith is the foundation of all religion. The
Athanasian creed was formulated with this idea."

"I prefer the Holy Word," said Tom, calmly

"In the Old Testament I find mention of one Lord or Jehovah, and the prediction that He will appear in human form on earth. In the New Testament I find mention of His appearance as Divine Humanity, thus fulfilling the prophecy; but I do not find anywhere in the Holy Scripture a concise or definite statement that God is more than one *person*. The Athanasian creed is another matter. It is of human origin and therefore imperfect and inaccurate. Stating first that the matter it treats of is mysterious, it goes on to explain the mystery, or pretends to, fails ignominiously, and finally declares that no one can be saved who does not believe in this explanation, which in itself is a tissue of absurd contradictions. It is worthy of the age in which it was written, and instead of making its author immortal, its very untruthfulness seems more apparent, from the fact that the author is not definitely known."

"St. Athanasius wrote the creed, I think," said the clergyman, quickly.

"It is not only quite certain that he did not write it," said Tom, "but there are many who attribute its authorship to Virgilius, a bishop from Africa."

"I never could read it with the slightest degree of patience," said Professor Romney. "It attempts to solve a mystery, fails completely, and then condemns or damns all who will not accept as infallible its imperfect explanation. Its texture is grossly human, and savors of the barbarism which tainted the age in which it was written."

"I admit," said Mr. Kendall,—and as he spoke the sea-serpent, seeming to make a desperate effort to escape, disappeared in the ample space between the clergyman's vest and coat,—"I admit that the creed is rather ambiguous and, perhaps, perplexing; but there are many clergymen who no longer pin their faith to it."

This signal retreat—we refer to that of the clergyman—drew a smile from more faces than one.

"*Sancta Maria, ora pro nobis,*" whispered Jack to Belle, while Tom, following up his advantage, said,—

"The fact, however, that doctrines change does not alter or affect basal truths. As the world advances in wisdom those doctrines which are no longer useful are thrown aside to be replaced by newer and brighter ones. This is the case with everything; supererogation is not a law of nature. Man's wants, both physical and mental, are supplied according to his actual need. This fact emphasizes the nobility and God-likeness of free determination.

"Physical wants are met according to the need of the hour and age. Invention is the outcome of a want, or, to put it more familiarly, ' Necessity

is the mother of invention.' The locomotive and
the old-fashioned stage-coach represent the necessities of two distinct ages. Electric light, gas,
lamp, and candle each represents the need of the
generation in which it served its greatest use."

The serpent had disappeared, and Tom waxed
eloquent as he continued,—

"It is the same with ideas and religious doctrines; those which lose their use fall back and
make room for newer and better.

" A doctrine flourishes just in proportion to the
quality of the soil in which its first seeds are sown.
That soil should be rich in love and faith. History and traditions are modified and completely
changed by time and repetition.

" Mythology is the fickle child of antiquity. The
myths of the Middle Ages show clearly how legends change by repetition and the hand of time.
St. George is claimed by nearly every nation on
the Eastern hemisphere. In Nabatæan mythology
he was Tammuz; in the Phœnician he was Adon;
in Syria, Baal; in Egypt, Osiris; in Arabia, El
Kouder or Tauz; and in our modern Christian
mythology he is the noble St. George who rescued the fair maiden; but it is conceded by good
authority that he had his real origin in the Shemitic
god Adonis, a name which signified the Lord. I
mention these facts to show that ancient legends
are modified to suit the ages in which they are

told, while the basal truths which underlie them
remain unchanged."

"We would soon be stranded upon the shore
of skepticism did we not possess faith," said Mr.
Kendall, in a determined manner.

"Granted," said Tom; "provided faith is
grounded in reason."

"Faith is the ground-work of love," said the
parson.

"I would reverse the proposition," said the
doctor, "putting love in the first place; but they
are in one sense inseparable and must work together. To love is to will, inasmuch as what we
will we love. If faith produced love and good
works, the great majority of professing Christians
would be noted for their charity and good deeds.
Is it so? Are not the clergy and great mass of
people deficient in this respect? Lack of charity
and love to the neighbor, it seems to me, stand
out prominently as defects to be remedied in the
church."

"True faith is inseparable from charity and love;
it is grounded in them."

"Why," asked Jack, whose equilibrium was now
restored by the disappearance of the sea-serpent,
—"why is it necessary for us to believe or have
faith in anything supernatural or transcendental?"

"Because," said Tom, after waiting in vain for
Mr. Kendall, the clergyman, to reply, "the mind

is the true instrument of the soul of man, which is in itself transcendental."

"But how will you prove your statement?" Jack said.

"The bare fact," replied Tom, thoughtfully, "that we are capable of a mental conception of a future life is positive proof that such a life exists. Let me explain more fully. It is impossible to think of a thing which does not exist. Try it. You may conceive of a centaur, to be sure, which as a centaur does not exist, but the horse's body and the man's head *are* realities which do exist, therefore the basis of your conception is tangible fact."

"But," said Jack, rather exultantly, "we get all of our ideas from nature, and not from any spirit-land that I am aware of."

"That's so," said Craik, laughing loudly, and waking up the major. "I never saw a ghost in my life, and never expect to."

"Nature," said Tom, slowly, and as if striving to reduce his thoughts to proper shape for the assimilation of moral dyspeptics,—"nature, as we see her in matter, is a great study; every particular thing in her three kingdoms has its substance, form, and use, and in this sense nature is a prefiguration of man. This law of prefiguration holds good throughout nature, and on it men have based their different theories of evolution. Each object

in nature prefigures something higher than itself
in the scale of perfection, until man is reached.
The frost upon the glass window prefigures vege-
tation, and the plant or tree, with its circulatory
apparatus and fibrous skeleton, prefigures the
animal."

"Yes," said the professor, interrupting; "I have
seen the *Ptilota plumòsa* remarkably pictured in
the frost-work; and in misty weather I have seen
upon the sidewalks frost-tracings which resembled
the foot-prints of certain aquatic birds, and upon
very thin ice I have noticed almost perfect repre-
sentations of some of the larger ferns, such as the
Polypodium aureum; but it never occurred to me
that these were prefigurations; the idea interests
me exceedingly. Pray proceed with your remarks,
doctor, for they seem to lead one's thoughts into
new fields."

"Yes," said Nettie, with true feeling; "do continue. The subject is intensely interesting."

Mr. Kendall politely bowed his desires, and
Tom proceeded,—

"I was simply about to state," said he, "that
the prefiguration of something higher or better is
apparent everywhere. The beautiful snow-flakes
show us lovely flowers, and also prefigure the
star-fish; but the most significant and beautiful
prefigurations are found in plants and flowers, as
the professor will tell you."

"Yes, indeed," said the professor, pleased at the opportunity to ventilate his knowledge; "there are plants which derive their names from their resemblance to higher forms in nature; and of course you are aware that plants and flowers sleep and eat, and the sensitive plant actually moves."

"I was about to answer the question as to how the fact of a higher life and power could be proved," said Tom. "Those prefigurations in the mineral and vegetable kingdoms are continued on a grander and higher scale in the animal kingdom, prefiguring there man's affections and intelligence. People recognize these latter prefigurations instinctively, as can be proved by the commonplace methods of speech. They say, for instance, that a man is '*as cross as a bear*,' '*as greedy as a pig*,' '*as obstinate as a mule*,' '*as gentle as a lamb*,' '*as gay as a lark*,' '*as harmless as a dove*,' and so on *ad infinitum;* they thus unconsciously, or wisely, if you will, acknowledge the prefigurations among the lower animals which represent the qualities in man. Now, to come directly to the point, all of these kingdoms of nature—the mineral, vegetable, and animal—prefigure or foretell the existence of a superior being, and we trace them up higher and higher in the wonderful scale until we reach man, the epitome of nature."

"Yes, that is clear," said the professor.

"Now," continued Tom, "what reason have we

for stopping here? We must study men and go higher still. We get our information from a true source that man is made in the image and likeness of his Creator, but this does not satisfy the skeptic; he must investigate to see if this statement is reasonable. He finds that man possesses a *free will,*—or freedom to act as he pleases; this suggests something God-like; it is, in fact, a prefiguration of God. This quality of freedom is referable to something in one which is apart from matter; it is spiritual; hence we find the soul or spirit of man, which also prefigures the ' Great Spirit,'—God. This spirit being superior to or above nature is transcendental; it is supernatural; and as it is destined to a life here on earth of probation or preparation, this life is, therefore, a prefiguration of a higher and a future existence."

" Your reasoning is good, sir," said the professor, enthusiastically, " and has more weight with me than all of the arguments on the Trinity and Resurrection, or treatises upon Redemption and the Atonement, that I have ever investigated. The trouble is they are not based on sound reason."

" I think," said Tom, " that modern thought is shaping itself to facts in harmony with those I have just stated."

" May I ask your ideas on the theory of evolution?" asked Mr. Kendall, graciously.

" Certainly," said the doctor, looking in Jack's

direction to see if he commanded his attention;
"but first let me remark that I claim no originality
in what I have stated."

"Allow me to ask," said Jack, who seemed to
have entirely forgotten the sea-serpent, "what
absolute proof have we of the existence of a
Divine Being?"

"I was about to speak of that," said Tom; "but
let me answer you in part by asking a question.
Is it not reasonable to suppose that all things were
in the beginning created? Or let me put the
question differently,—Is it rational to believe that
anything can be created out of or from nothing?
Is such a supposition reasonable?"

"Certainly not," said the professor, answering
for Jack. "Everything possesses substance, form,
and power or use, and those qualities could not
emanate from nothing, which, according to our
conception, is void. It would be as reasonable to
suppose that a vacuum could produce a hurri-
cane."

"Well, then," said Tom, smiling his approval
at the professor, who was becoming an enthusiastically, "we arrive at the reasonable conclusion
that all things were created by some agency or
person; and since the analogies of the lower
kingdoms point to man, the grand macrocosm,
including man, points to a being capable of producing it. Such a being must, of course, be om-

nipotent, omniscient, and omnipresent, and such is
our conception by natural processes of God, the
Creator of the universe."

"That is a well-worn theory," said Mr. Kendall,
cheerfully. "We judge of God by His works just
as we judge in the same manner of man. If a
carpenter, for instance, does good work we know
he is a good carpenter, if we only see his work;
in the same way we judge of God. It is not
necessary for us to have ocular demonstration;
we feel and realize His greatness and goodness
without, by the wonderful adjustment of all things
in nature."

"But you were about to give us your ideas on
the evolution theory," said Mr. Van Dusen, who
had been secretly wondering what had become of
the minister's sea-serpent.

"In the first place," said Tom, smiling, "it is
only fair to tell you all frankly that I differ from
the majority of the advocates of continuous evolution from Anaximander to Huxley. They all
or nearly so, if I am correctly informed, have ad-
hered to the belief that changes in what they term
the 'chain of nature' occur continuously; from a
state of inferiority to one of superiority. This I
claim would be impossible. An inferior thing or
being cannot create a thing or being superior to
itself."

"True," said the professor, excitedly, slapping

the table with his bony hand; "that is a grand
thought." Then, suddenly becoming serious again,
he asked, "But how then, doctor, can a race of
beings improve their condition as we, for instance,
in this country are improving? How can we do
this without external help?"

"We cannot," said Tom, smiling at the professor's enthusiasm. "The same Being who created
us is continually improving our spiritual condition.
You must have remarked that Christianity and
mental improvement always travel together. The
chain of nature or, more properly speaking, system of nature, which evolutionists claim is continuous, is in a measure analogous to a musical scale.
In music the notes must be discrete to be har-
monious or concordant. A continuous scale of
music would sound like a shriek or an Indian war-
whoop. It is the same with colors, which, by the
way, correspond beautifully to the musical scale.
A painting would have no character unless the
colors were discrete. It would, like the war-
whoop, be inharmonious. The same rule holds
good in the grand system of nature from the
highest (man) to the lowest kingdom. Each kind
or species is discrete, and must be so to harmonize
with and fit into its distinct or specific place in the
universe. If the highest quadrupeds terminated
with the monkey, the lion would lose his crown
and sceptre. The eagle is on another discrete

13*

plane. He is the acknowledged king of birds, and with him superiority in the feathered tribe ends."

" I clearly get your idea," said the professor; " and you have demolished a famous castle in the air which I have been building for years. Your theory leaves one satisfied, while that of continuous evolution does not harmonize with Bible teaching or with apparent natural laws."

" No, indeed," said the clergyman; " and I am afraid the missing link will never be found."

Van Dusen, who with the rest had been an amused and attentive listener, and at the same time a little anxious, since the sudden and mysterious disappearance of the sea-serpent, lest the conversation might become tiresome to some of them, here spoke, saying kindly,—

" Doctor, I have known you incidentally for several years; but I never dreamed that you were the treasure-house of so much good philosophy. One would think that the onerous duties of caring for the sick would be as much as you could possibly attend to."

" Well," said Tom, laughing, "as for philosophy, I admit that it is good; but the ideas which I have expressed are by no means original with me; and as for caring for the sick I must say that I, for the present at least, deny the charge, for I never had the pleasure of sitting at table with

more healthy people, and, I desire to add, with
more congenial friends."

Shortly after this, Mr. Van Dusen suggested
that they should all adjourn to the deck, where
he promised the gentlemen a comforting cigar and
the ladies a cool breeze.

On their way up the narrow companion-way to
the deck Jack found time to say to Belle,—
"Your brother has toppled over my house with
his radical ideas."

"I am glad of it," said Belle, pleasantly, "if it
was built upon sand;" and Tom, as he assisted
Miss Knowles to ascend, saw in her beautiful eyes
a look which he had never seen there before,
and which thrilled his honest heart with joy.
The conviction forced itself upon him, then and
there, that his heart was no longer his own, and
he felt that supreme gladness which comes to
man but once in a lifetime. He pressed the hand
he held tenderly, and in a low, earnest voice
said,—

"I am afraid I neglected you at dinner. I——"

"Oh, no, indeed," she replied, quickly interrupting him and correctly interpreting his affectionate
tone and manner. "You made me proud of you,
—of knowing you," she added, blushing at the
thought of her proprietorship in him and modestly
fearing that she might have gone too far. After
seating themselves, Tom was called aside for some

purpose by Mr. Van Dusen, and Mr. Craik took
the vacated camp-chair at Nettie's side.

" Is the odor of tobacco offensive to you, Miss
Knowles ?" he asked, as he accepted a cigar which
was passed to him.

" No," replied Nettie ; " I do not mind it much
in the open air. Tell me, Mr. Craik, why do men
smoke ?"

" That is a question difficult to answer intelligently," he replied, laughing. " If I were to tell
you because it is a pleasure, you would probably
ask, why a pleasure ? if I were to tell you because
it is a necessity, you would probably puzzle me by
asking, why a necessity ? and my answers to these
inquiries might not satisfy you, or you would accuse me of joking. The truth is both reasons are
correct. We smoke at first because others whom
we admire or respect have done so before us ; their
example stimulates us to the trial. There are dis-
agreeable reminiscences connected with the first
few attempts ; after which we smoke because, as I
said before, it becomes a necessity, a habit, which
is so fastened upon us that we cannot easily renounce it,—we are in one sense slaves ; then, as to
the pleasure, to be very frank with you, that is the
greatest when we have been the longest deprived
of indulgence of the habit ; tobacco being a powerful narcotic, it quiets the nerves and soothes the
mind until it is time to smoke again."

"Your answer is frank at any rate," Nettie replied; "but it seems to me, were I a man, I would allow no habit to so fasten upon me as to involve my freedom."

"That is a matter about which very wise heads have differed for many years," said Tom, who, having returned and thrown himself at Nettie's feet, now joined in the conversation. "You are and have been a slave to several habits which are a necessity to you,—eating, drinking, breathing, etc."

"But," said Nettie, who was by no means weak in an argument, "I was referring to habits which are acquired, and not the legitimate necessities of life, which of course are indispensable."

"It is a deep subject," said Tom, puffing his cigar with evident enjoyment. "As babes we live upon the simplest diet; later on we mature, we acquire the habits of digesting solid foods; we also acquire habits of neatness, order, truthfulness, etc., and their opposites."

"I will not be rude enough to say that smoking is one of the opposites," said Nettie; "but these acquired habits which you have mentioned are healthful and in harmony with hygienic laws, whereas it requires a struggle on the part of nature to become accustomed, if she ever does, to the poisonous effects of tobacco."

Tom, who had been cleverly drawing Nettie out, now changed his tactics.

"You are quite right, Miss Knowles; there is a great difference between a habit which fulfils a requirement of nature and one which taxes its endurance. I do not desire to become a champion of the habit of using tobacco, or any other poison."

"Then why are you, who believe example to be of more importance than precept, one of the great army of tobacco-users?"

"I could easily desert its ranks," said Tom, throwing his freshly-lighted Havana over the taffrail of the yacht into the water. "There will be a short struggle and a victory."

"Do you mean to say that you can and will give up using tobacco?" asked Nettie, now somewhat frightened at her own bravery.

"Yes," said Tom. "Since you have so fairly beaten me, its defender, tobacco shall no longer have charms for me; but I have long had this move in contemplation, for, as a physician, I know too well its evil effects."

"I know an old man ninety-five years of age, who is hale and hearty, and who has used tobacco all of his life," said Mr. Craik, with a slight sneer.

"That may be true, if you are a physician and have examined him," said Tom; "but the probabilities are that he has his ills and ails, and that the vigorous constitution which has been able to stand the effects of the poison so long would have been still more vigorous had he never used the weed.

"The tobacco-heart is as familiar to men of my profession as the rheumatism. To be sure, we do not know just how the poison affects the action of the heart, except as we conjecture through the pernicious effects upon the blood. Microscopic investigation shows us a decided depletion, by disintegration of the red corpuscles, and an anæmic heart invariably follows. That is about all we know about it; but that should be enough to cure a physician of smoking."

"Some men stand this poison a good many years," said Craik, fondling his cigar.

"True," said Tom, turning so that he could see Craik fairly; "some men seem to thrive upon the poisons of this world just as some seem to flourish in sin. I have no desire to emulate people who continually defy nature."

"Well," said Nettie, inwardly delighted at Tom's great strength of character, "Dr. Tillottson, if you are sure that my influence does not cause you to renounce this pleasure, I am glad to see you give up smoking; but I should prefer to see you smoke rather than to feel that I was the means of causing you any inconvenience or unhappiness.

"Why, here comes a boat with a little boy in it!"

"Yes," said Craik; "it is the boy from Oldport with the New York papers. Van Dusen has them sent to him regularly."

The boy threw the Sunday papers on board, and they were courteously passed to the ladies, who began to read little scraps of information aloud to the gentlemen. Nettie, after reading a variety of little notices, stumbled upon the following, which she read to Craik and Tom:

"Not captured yet. The supposed murderer of Rogers, the wealthy Roman banker, is still at large, and has been traced to this country by able detectives, who are employed by relatives and friends of the deceased. It is hoped they will be successful in their search, as he is a desperate character and an old offender, who, it is said, is wanted in England for several offences of a criminal nature, including the Thames Bank robbery, which occurred two years ago. He was known in Rome as Antoinne De Lacey, but claimed to be an Englishman. In England he went by the name of James Bolan, or among his pals as Gentleman Jim; and there he claimed American birth and parentage. It is rumored that he was implicated in, if not the author of, the great Capette forgery last year in Paris."

"What a rascal he must be," said Tom.

"Yes," said Craik, "but they won't catch him; they never catch such clever scamps."

"What dreadful things they put in the papers," said Nettie, sorry that she had read the paragraph.

Has the reader ever contemplated the vast power which surges behind the daily press? It lies not so much in the many items of news which we find there, as in the mighty influence upon the human mind through the suggestions of myriads of ideas. A newspaper is a bonanza of thought. Let us look into one briefly; there seems to be enough food for contemplation. Advertisements which suggest poverty, sin, and suffering. The events of yesterday which occurred, perhaps, upon the other side of the globe. Information of vessels supposed to have been lost at sea; accidents upon the railroads; accounts of joyous weddings and sad funerals; cases at law, just and unjust; wants of all descriptions; noted arrivals and departures; rumors of wars abroad, and verbatim accounts of the proceedings of our own Congress. How hungry this monster called the "Press" is. Every item of news, no matter how important or insignificant, finds ready access to its terrible maw.

The newspaper is literary bread for the poor man; cheap mental food which is growing more and more wholesome as the world advances in knowledge and improves in morals.

Newspapers may be compared to schoolmasters; some are narrow and so ill tempered that the switch is their main dependence; others are calm, dignified, and intellectual, winning meritorious success by moral suasion.

The career of the former class is lively and short-lived; while the latter naturally become the permanent pets of the public. The former overstep legal boundaries, suffer punishment, and perish; while the latter, by justice and conservatism, gain power as they distribute knowledge. We think that the newspapers of the future are destined to become the medium by which human interests are united in a common unselfishness.

During Nettie's reading of the above article, Craik had appeared ill at ease; and had she glanced up at his face as she finished she would have noticed his agitation and have taken alarm at his appearance; but she calmly drifted on to another article.

It happened also that Tom, who was looking at Nettie, failed to observe his appearance, and shortly afterward Craik, excusing himself, retired to the cabin to write letters as he said, and they saw no more of him that day. Mr. Van Dusen, in his genteel way, made himself very agreeable to the entire party. He was always ready to supply fuel to a lagging conversation, and never intruded his ideas when there was no apparent demand for them. His remarks, too, were so sprinkled with a vein of honest good-humor that his guests were charmed with him. He invited them all for a long

ocean sail upon the "Siren," and named the following Tuesday as the day, thoughtfully extending
the invitation to Mrs. Tillottson and her sister.
The invitation was gladly accepted by all present,
and shortly afterward Tom and his friends took
their departure, as it was their intention to call
upon his mother before returning to Cup Island.

"What a delightful man Mr. Van Dusen is,"
said Belle, on their way to Oldport.

"He is, indeed," said Jack; "he exercises such
excellent taste and judgment in the entertainment
of his guests. I shall never forget how delicate
he was about asking the price of a picture which
he bought of me last fall; he saw it at the academy
exhibition."

"Yes, I remember it well," said Belle; "it was
Beatrice, was it not? It was at the academy that
I first met Mr. Van Dusen. For a millionaire, he
certainly is remarkably considerate and unselfish."

"I do not exactly understand," said Jack, "how
he and Craik became intimate, they are so very
different."

"Van Dusen says he was introduced to Craik
at his hotel in New York," said Tom.

CHAPTER VIII.

Mrs. Tillottson moves to Cup Island—Bid as an Angler—The
. Oldport Church—Mr. Kendall as a Philanthropist—Jack deeply
Impressed—The Sermon—The Serenade.

MRS. TILLOTTSON received the party with open
arms and a beaming countenance. Almost her
first remark was, " Girls, we are coming over to
the cottage to live ; I am so much better that I
feel perfectly able to do so. I have engaged a
carpenter to make a few improvements so that we
can all be accommodated and comfortable. I cannot endure being here almost alone any longer,
and my appetite is getting so ravenous that I
should think Mrs. Sandy would be glad to see me
go."

Nettie and Belle were delighted at this piece of
news, and the young men showed their pleasure
by offering to do all sorts of little favors if Mrs.
Tillottson carried out her resolution.

"We attended church here this morning," she
continued, "and heard a Mr. Kendall. He is not
their regular pastor; I believe they have none,
but he gave a very simple and instructive lesson,
and I was much impressed by his sincerity and
earnestness ; but you must now tell us all about

your day upon the island and your dinner on the yacht."

This they did at once, informing her that Mr. Kendall was one of the yachting party and was present at the dinner.

" There is to be a service at the little church again this evening, and he is to preach," said Mrs. Tillottson.

" Let us all come over and go," said Nettie.

This was agreed to, and saying good-by to Mrs. Tillottson they started for home, as it was now late in the afternoon.

" I wonder how Bid has passed the day ?" said Belle to Nettie, as they were being rowed over the smooth water to Cup Island.

" I hope she has not tried any more boating experiments," said Nettie, laughing.

" There is no danger of that," said Jack; " she is too much in mortal terror of the ' moanin' say.' "

On arriving at the cottage, however, Bid was nowhere to be seen. They hunted the house over without finding her; then they went to the summer-house, thinking that perhaps she had been caught there, as they had, by the tide, but no Bid was to be seen. Matters began to look serious. The table was carefully laid for tea, the kettle was cheerily singing in the fireplace, and there was wood crackling on the fire, showing that Bid could not long have been absent from the cottage; but the island was small, and they had not succeeded in finding her, so they began to get apprehensive. Jack left them and went on a tour of inspection alone. Soon he was seen returning from the direction of North Rock and at the same time beckoning them to come. Following his lead they at last found Bid sitting on the sea side of North Rock, with a fishing-rod lying beside her, fast asleep. The narrow ledge upon which she was sitting or reclining, with her head resting against the shelving wall, was so precariously situated that Jack had not awakened her, fearing that she would be startled and fall into the water, some fifteen feet below. There was a short consultation as to the best method of arousing her, and it was at last decided that it should be by music. They therefore began singing in very low tones one of their favorite quartettes. Gradually increasing the volume of sound, they were soon singing at the tops of their voices; but Bid seemed to be charmed by the music into deeper and heavier slumber, until they, reaching the end of their song, looked at each other, puzzled as to how they could accomplish their design without giving Bid a bath in the briny deep.

"We must get a rope around her," said Tom; "for if she should drop into the water she would drown; it is very deep there."

Jack rushed back to the cottage and brought a

long, new clothes-line; then the two young men, by tying the end of the clothes-line to a fish-line, dexterously slipping a fish-pole under Bid, then tying a slip-knot in such a way that it formed a noose, soon had poor Bid so secured that they could hold her up by hanging on to the other end of the line.

"Now," said Jack, in a low tone, "all take hold of the line, so; that's it. Now hold tight and I will call her."

"Bid! Oh, Bid!"

Bid opened her eyes quickly, and, seeing herself between heaven and water, gave a start and slid off of the ledge, just as they had feared and expected; but the rope tightening, they held her dangling, screaming, and kicking just above the water. Jack roared, and Tom could not help laughing; but the girls were frightened, for the strain upon their arms as Bid's by no means feather weight tightened the rope was not easy for them to endure.

"Tom, do hurry and pull her up," said Belle. "I can't hold on any longer."

"All right," said Tom. "Jack and I can hold her; you two can let go," which they did.

"Bid," said Tom, shouting over the edge of the rock,—"Bid, is that you down there?"

"Oh, Misther Tarm! Misther Tarm!" screamed Bid, at the top of her voice; "oi thought oi was dead entirely. Sure, an' is it you, your dear self, Misther Tarm, or am oi drameing the wurest drame of me loife?"

"What are you doing down there?" shouted Tom.

"Sure, it's meeself that don't know," said Bid. "Oh, Misther Tarm, save me, save me from the depths av the moanin' say!"

"Let's pull her up," said Jack, who was laughing so hard that he feared his strength might suddenly leave him.

"All right," said Tom; "pull away." But it was not as easy as they had imagined; for by the time they had fairly landed Bid on top of North Rock they were both out of breath and nearly exhausted, poor Bid being almost dead with fright and probably bruised in more places than one. The girls delivered her from the embrace of the clothes-line, explanations followed, and they all returned to the cottage.

"Sure, oi was troing me luck at the fish an' felled ashleep entirely," said Bid.

In the evening, shortly after tea, they took the little boat again and returned to Oldport, walking to the little church, which stood upon a country road not far from the post-office. It was not an imposing-looking edifice, and, save a long shed for the accommodation of horses, it stood alone. The building was of wood, plain, and square, with a small steeple and belfry on one end of the roof, which, as our friends drew near, was sending forth the doleful notes of a cracked bell, while on the inside of the door-way below a stoop-shouldered young man of cadaverous mien was producing the sounds by vigorous pulls upon a bell-rope. On the wooden steps leading to the church stood and sat, in little groups, a number of the village swains, dressed in clothes to which they evidently were but one-seventh accustomed.

Tom and Nettie led the way into the building, noticing as they entered a powerful odor of kerosene, which was given off by the two or three old-fashioned lamps suspended by wires from the ceiling; and their steps, as they tramped over the bare boards of the floor, sounded hollow and loud, attracting the curious attention of the few people already assembled.

After they were fairly seated upon a wooden bench, cushionless, and with a back which touched only at one point near the shoulders, and had become somewhat accustomed to the staring match which ensued, they were able to make a few mental notes of their surroundings. The apartment was, perhaps, forty feet long from door to pulpit, and thirty feet the other way. In it were two rows of straight-backed wooden benches, while facing the audience, and to the left of the pulpit, which, by the way, consisted of a table

somewhat resembling an old-fashioned wash-stand,
were two benches upon which sat the choir. The
choir consisted of six members. The leader, a
man of perhaps fifty-three or fifty-four summers,
was immediately recognized by our friends as Mr.
Sandy, the postmaster. Beside him, upon the
same bench, sat a middle-aged woman dressed in a
gown of sage-green color, and ornamented at the
neck by a large pink bow. She was of fair complexion, puffy cheeks, and tapered rather con-
spicuously from her hips to the narrow tip of her
conical straw hat. To the observer in front her
position was apparently not a secure one, for as
her feet failed to reach the church-floor she
seemed in imminent danger of sliding off the
bench. We will quiet the anxiety of the reader
by the assurance that no such calamity occurred.
This lady and Mr. Sandy, who were evidently the
leading vocalists, were busily engaged in consultation over a hymn-book and in dictating to their
companions upon the bench.

At last notice having been given to sing the one
hundred and sixty-third hymn by Mr. Kendall,
who had arrived and taken his seat at the wash-
stand, the choir arose; Mr. Sandy fumbled in his
vest-pocket awhile, finally producing a tuning-fork,
which he tapped sharply against the heel of his
boot, and taking the cue from that he began in a
harsh voice to lead the choir.

We will not attempt to describe the music which
followed. The sentiment of the hymn was good.
Perhaps the verbiage might have been a little extravagant: we remember something about "bleed-
ing hearts," "conquering heroes," "golden streets,"
and "bowels yearning," and the superlatives might
have been a trifle numerous; but adjectives are a
great resource in the country, particularly in a
country church. The music we pass over with a
sigh. There are moments in the lives of all which
cannot be lived over perfectly in words. Our
friends were too much overcome to add their
voices to the harmony; besides, they were un-
familiar with the air. Not so, however, the
vigorous congregation; they sang as though they
thought they never would be allowed that blessed
privilege again; opening their by no means delicate
mouths to their fullest extent, they emitted a
volume of sound which seemed to almost loosen
the rafters of the edifice.

Jack was visibly affected; the corners of his
mouth were restless, twitching spasmodically, and
Belle, his neighbor, who noticed the evident emotion, was in painful apprehension lest he should
audibly give vent to his pent-up feelings, when
suddenly the music ceased, the people subsided
into their seats, there was the customary rustling
of dresses, scuffling of feet, and clearing of
throats, until Mr. Kendall rising from his chair,

and thereby commanding silence, quietly began his address.

The sermon was a friendly talk rather than an elaborate essay, and our listeners gave Mr. Kendall great credit for discretion on this occasion. He tried to show the simple, hard-working people before him the intimate connection between God and His works. He likened the roaring of the sea to the voice of the Almighty warning sinners to repent ere it was too late; quite a novel and practical comparison, and one which was no doubt remembered by some of the fishermen present to their advantage. He dwelt upon the generous goodness of God, as evidenced by the ease with which man may stretch forth his hand and be fed and clothed. " He may drop," said he, "a line into the sea and it will bring forth the nourishing fish, or he may drop a seed into the soil, and it will bring forth the succulent fruit, such is the thoughtfulness of divine Providence. God, however, is impatient of the slothful man and will not abide the man who is sinful. He has given us a few laws to govern our conduct toward each other and Himself; if we observe these laws, which you all know are the Ten Commandments, we shall all reach heaven."

It was a simple discourse, delivered in a frank, brotherly manner, and it was easy to see that it made the right impression. Our friends were somewhat surprised at the absence of arrogance, so noticeable at dinner upon the " Siren." Jack was pleased with the minister's way of talking to the Oldport people, and liked him better for the sincerity which was so evident in his manner. Mr. Kendall, like all poor mortals, had his faults, but he was a worker.

Some very worthy people, most valuable too in the busy bustle of the world, make a poor appearance at a dinner. Mr. Kendall's mission in the world was to do good. He did it. Among plain folks he was at his ease. Highly educated and reared in refinement, he seldom found it difficult when in intercourse with people below him in mental culture to adopt a manner appropriate to the spirit of his subject and his listener. This he did naturally and without thought, because policy was as foreign to his nature as was the inception and assimilation of some of Tom's radical ideas. He was a man of ruts. Tom's theories fell like seed in a sandy and unfertile soil; they were not indigenous, and therefore could not flourish. They produced glimmerings of light in his mental horizon for the time being, which were welcomed as the eye greets pyrotechnics, but like the pyrotechnics they fleeted away, and time soon obliterated most of their glory, leaving only a pleasant recollection.

Mr. Kendall's apparent arrogance at the dinner

was simply the reflex action of an attempt to appear natural. He was nervously anxious upon the subjects which were discussed, feeling in a measure responsible for whatever results might accrue. To battle with pyrrhonism or calmly dissect religious dogmas which had imbued his mind for years was impossible.

The world is full of similar minds. Our theological seminaries are annually turning out hundreds of such young men with the college curriculum frozen into the very marrow of their ethical bones; wholesale thinking-machines from a common pattern, warranted to turn out other thinking-machines by the simple turning of a lingual crank; young men who learn surface-logic and mental science by a stencil process, a sort of photographic manual, consisting of a positive college faculty and a negative diploma-seeker. Will the present optional departure ameliorate this machine system? Let us wait patiently and see. Perhaps it is a step in the right direction; it is certainly God's method of dealing with His children. Why should not we hold as hallowed the precious will of man?

"What is your opinion of the sermon?" Belle asked of Jack, as they strolled along the moon-lit road in the direction of Oldport.

"It reminded me," said Jack, between the puffs of a permitted cigar, "it reminded me of a well-drawn study of a sunset at sea in gray. Color was lacking, but the simple outlines were good."

"But did you notice the rapt attention and respectful deference which Mr. Kendall seemed to command from the Oldport people?" asked Belle.

"Yes, indeed," replied Jack, "and no doubt the plain truths sank deeply and for the first time into some of their souls; but, you see, I am not a native of Oldport, and Mr. Kendall was not aiming his shafts at me. I need color. Now, Tom's remarks to-day at dinner were full of color and brilliancy, and they were so fresh and new that my very soul was stirred and thirsts now for more. He has never forced his opinions upon me, or I might have laughed at them; but when I saw how thoroughly they harmonized with the naturalistic knowledge of Professor Romney, how they seemed to formulate or open out a new science of ethics, which might justly be called Physico-theology; how in accepting religion one may cling all the more dutifully to science and art; my very heart was touched and I loved the dear boy more than ever. You must indeed be proud of such a brother."

"It is doubly pleasant," said Belle, who felt tears in her eyes, "to hear my brother spoken of so affectionately, and you can rest assured that Tom is equally ardent in his affection for you, for there are no half-way stations in his heart, although

by nature he is not perhaps quite so demonstra-
tive."

"It is strange," said Jack, after a short pause,
during which the stillness of the Sabbath evening
was unbroken save by the pattering of their feet
upon the roadway and the industrious music of
the insect world. "I have been somewhat of a
reader, and have partially digested the majority of
our modern writers; but the web of philosophy
which I had woven was completely carried away
before the little puff of wisdom from Tom's noddle
to-day.   It is very strange."

"No, not so very strange," said Belle, feelingly;
"for Tom has also been an industrious reader, and
he has imbibed a great many of his ideas from my
father, who was a man very much like Tom."

"What struck me as sublime," Jack replied,
"was that idea of prefiguration which he advanced. The figurative language of nature is so
very apparent, it so fills and satisfies the desires of
the soul, that it is unconsciously acknowledged by
the great masses of humanity, both in their speech
and actions.   I suppose that the very words of
language were borrowed by man from nature in
some way as a means of expressing his thoughts."

"Yes," said Tom, who with Nettie was now
close behind them and had overheard Jack's last
words; "I have no doubt of it, for the sounds of
certain words are identical with those we hear in

nature. We speak of the coo of a dove, for instance. Here *coo* is the very sound which the dove makes. It is the same with the *mew* of a kitten, the *twitting* of the birds, the *caw* of a crow, the *roar* of a lion, the *hiss* of a serpent, the *babble* of a brook, and so on *ad infinitum*. Some birds and animals are named from the sounds which ͵they produce,—the *pee-wee*, for instance, or the *whippoorwill, humming*-bird, etc."

"If it is a fact," said Jack, "that we borrow all of our ideas from nature——"

"Oh, no," interrupted Tom; "it is not so; we no doubt have borrowed sounds from nature to express our thoughts, but it is not so always; with ideas it is different. An idea is spiritual; it is more subtle; it is superior to nature; nevertheless each particular thing or object in nature has its corresponding spiritual idea."

"Can you illustrate that statement?" said Jack, somewhat doubtingly.

"Certainly," said Tom. "I say that every phenomenon or all combined phenomena in nature— and the combinations are infinite—are but correspondences of spiritual ideas; for instance, animals may be divided into two kinds: those which are gentle and harmless and those which are ferocious and dangerous. The former, we readily see, are correspondences of our ideas (spiritual) of goodness; the very words gentle and harmless are

ideas.   A lamb, we say, is gentle; a dog reminds
us of faithfulness, the dove of innocence or love,
and so on.   On the other hand, the vicious animals correspond to phases contrary to goodness,
or phases of evil.   You would hesitate to say that
a man was as good as a wolf, or as gentle as a
hyena, for these animals both correspond to evil
ideas; you would say instead that he was as gentle
as a lamb, or if you did not get your correspondence from the animal kingdom in nature, you
would choose it from the vegetable or mineral, in
which case you would say that the man was as
honest or true as steel.   Young ladies are said to
be sweet as roses."

"I begin to get your meaning," said Jack.
"Man is in a sort of equilibrium between good
and evil, and by his freedom of will may choose
the one or the other."

"Exactly," said Tom.   "The natural around us
is a perfect correspondence—but on a lower plane
—of the spiritual world, and man is in equilibrium
between them.   This equilibrium is, as you have
hinted, his freedom or his free will; his body is
on the natural plane, but his soul is spiritual, on
a higher plane.   He is constantly surrounded with
things evil and good, but, being in equilibrium, he
has the power to choose only that which suits his
tastes; an evil man chooses evil things, a good
man good things."

"Why was he not made with power only to choose the good things?" asked Jack.

"Animals or the brutes of creation are so made," said Tom; "but man is made king of them all by virtue of his free will."

"Then, why is it that he falls?" said Jack.

"Because he possesses freedom of choice," said Tom. "He is made after the image of his Maker, with free determination, and therefore he is led, not forced, by the Lord, through conscience, only up to that point where his freedom would be interfered with. A horse has no freedom."

"I think it is clear to me now," said Jack.

"It was always clear to me," said Nettie. "I was taught to put my trust in divine Providence, but have always known that it was in my power to break the commandments if I so desired."

"You women are different from men in many respects," said Jack. "Sometimes it will take a man years to master a single thought which a woman will imbibe by intuition in a moment."

"Perhaps that is so," said Nettie; "but it is certain, I think, that women cannot so readily put their thoughts or intuitions, as you call them, into words; of course, I mean on the serious subjects of life."

"That may be," said Jack, laughing, "because words after all are very superficial, and inadequately express our ideas."

We hope the reader will not form a poor opinion of the doctor. He was, like a great many other young men of his day, given to the serious contemplation of subjects about which, perhaps, it were as well if some men did not think at all. His mind was so constituted that it wanted a reason for all things. If an atheist said, "There is no God," Tom would respect his assertion only so far as the atheist could back it up by good reasoning; if an agnostic insisted that men have no right to freely assert a belief in the supernatural and spiritual, Tom would accuse him of the very positivism which he condemned in others, and by which he claimed a title to the name agnostic. Pessimism shared a like fate under Tom's rigid cross-examination. He believed in a perfect God, as impartial as the sun is with its rays, and as constant; as the earth turns away from the sun, so Tom believed that men turn away from God, the immutable.

Perhaps he would have made as good a lawyer as he did a physician, although he applied the same method in the diagnosis of disease,—viz., judgment by exclusion.

There are some who think that this faculty of weighing carefully every logical conclusion is, in a young man, an unpardonable assumption. We know a venerable old gentleman, long and deeply studied in mental science, who will not listen patiently to an argument which does not begin by assuming as true a "fundamental principle" with which he is familiar or in concord. Now, Tom would probably dig away at these fundamental principles or foundations until he had reached the bottom and satisfied himself that there were no flaws there. Can we blame him for this? On the contrary, we are inclined to indulge the boy in his hobby; it may in time lead him into fields of real wisdom, public lands overflowing with the milk and honey of erudition. By timid steps the infant pedestrians first totter upon their mother-earth, yet how indulgent we are with the little darlings in their scamperings; how well we know that encouragement is all they want, in order, some day, to become expert upon their feet. Let us indulge Tom; he will grow in time beyond the feeble efforts which we now see him making. He is tottering in the right direction, and after all, dear reader, are we not all totterers in the great mother-world of ideas? Now let us rejoin our young people.

The night was perfect, the air redolent with the sweet odor of new-mown hay; the clear light of the moon, the lively incessant chorus of insect voices, and the anthems of the frogs, all of these things seemed to raise their spirits as they strolled homeward along the winding country road.

It was equally delightful on the harbor. As they pulled the boat past the "Siren" they sang a beautiful quartette serenade, and were vigorously applauded by the party of yachtsmen.

Then the gentlemen on the "Siren" endeavored to return the compliment by singing a chorus, ignominiously failed, but nevertheless were heartily applauded by our young friends in the row-boat.

Mr. Van Dusen shouted from the yacht, "Ship a-ho-oo-y!"

"Hello there!" shouted Jack, with his vigorous young voice, in reply.

"Lay to and show your colors!" said Van Dusen.

"Ay, ay, sir, lay to she is!" screamed Tom.

"What ship is that, and where bound?" somebody shouted from the yacht.

"This is the 'Pigmy'!" Belle screamed in reply. "From Ancientville, bound for the happy land o' Caanan with a cargo of mammoths! Who are you?"

But the reply came to them so faintly, owing to a puff of wind from a contrary direction, that it was lost upon the waters and they heard it not. As they proceeded, however, on their course to the island, a beautiful rocket, shot over their heads and bursting high in the zenith, sent an expansive spray of colored sparks slowly drifting above them, and mingling a thousand bright reflections with the shimmering moonlight upon the waters below. Then, at a signal from Jack, they gave three rousing cheers for the "Siren," which were heartily returned from the yacht, when stillness once more reigned upon the pretty bay, and Neptune's kingdom was allowed to sleep in peace. Thus ended happily their first Sunday upon Cup Island.

CHAPTER IX.

Mr. Dexter's Condition improves—Augustus Campion—A Successful Lawyer—Employing a Detective—Mr. Bangs sails for Europe—Ferris and his Labors—Mr. Dexter able to write.

As time dragged slowly on with Mr. Dexter, his condition gradually but slowly improved; his physician gave him daily encouragement, holding out hopes of his ultimate recovery, provided he avoided all undue excitement and exertion. He had already quite recovered the use of his hands and arms, but his speech still continued so imperfect that he was obliged to write all of his communications and desires upon a slate. About a week after his affliction his nurse, a young lady of pleasing manners and appearance, was reading to him from a newspaper, when she happened upon the same article which we have heard his niece read to Mr. Craik and Tom on board of the "Siren." Mr. Dexter was greatly excited when she finished and motioned for the slate, writing upon it his desire to see his lawyer, Mr. Campion, at once.

Augustus Campion, LL.D., senior partner of the firm of Campion & Bangs, sat at his desk industriously formulating a brief. Half buried in papers, he seemed to know by instinct just where each one could be found; some were piled upon his desk in front of him, some were pigeon-holed to the right, some to the left, while a huge collection lay indiscriminately upon the broad window-sill at his elbow. He was a man of enormous stature, square of shoulders, and large-limbed. At first glance he reminded the observer of a huge mastiff of dangerous aspect, but closer scrutiny revealed a mildness in his deep blue eyes, an amiable expression about his mouth, which perpetually smiled, which soon put such a notion to shameful flight.

An irresistible agency drew one toward this colossus. His mild eyes carrying in them a gaze of interested inquiry, the cordial grasp of his warm, dry hand, and the assuring welcome which characterized the mellow tones of his voice, were sure to charm his visitor into an unconscious admiration of the man.

Mr. Campion had the reputation of being the best cross-questioner in the State. An obstinate witness, no matter how hostile when first put upon the stand, soon became friendly toward this huge mass of good-nature in spite of himself. His smile was worth a dozen bribes to a jury. It may therefore be inferred that Mr. Campion was a successful man. Yes, Mr. Campion was successful, for in addition to his power as a court lawyer he was a cool and level-headed thinker; but the real, the main reason for his success was his conscientiousness. He never hesitated to refuse to defend injustice, cruelty, dishonesty, or crime. Those were qualities which he would not tolerate in a client; but he was ever ready and eager to enter the lists against them, and thus he acquired a reputation for fairness and skill which brought the firm of Campion & Bangs as much business as they could well attend to.

Such was the man in whom Mr. Dexter had placed his trust. Slow to give advice until he had carefully sifted all the points in evidence, none could be more energetic when action was imperative or more prompt in emergencies. Let us accompany him to the bedside of his friend.

He found Mr. Dexter much better than he had seemed at his last visit, a few days previous. Mr. Dexter had given him Mr. Wigand's letter on a former occasion, and had instructed him to correspond with the attorneys at Rome in whose hands was the settlement of young Dexter's estate; now he showed him the newspaper article, which the lawyer read through carefully.

"Yes," he said, "I saw the same account in yesterday morning's paper."

Mr. Dexter then took his slate and wrote,—

"I want to employ detectives and hunt this rascal down."

Mr. Campion meditated a moment. "If he has escaped to this country," said he, "I think he will probably be found in New York City, or in some one of our large cities. If that is the case, one good detective will soon find him. There is a Chicago man, a detective, whom I have employed before, by the name of Ferris. He is very careful, and an expert; if you think best I will employ him at once."

"I do," wrote Mr. Dexter; "but do you think one man will be sufficient?"

"Yes, indeed," said the lawyer. "You know there are English detectives on his track already. The New York police are also on the lookout for him, and I am informed that Wigand, your son's partner, has offered a large reward for his capture. Ferris has had a long experience in tracking criminals, and I think he is just the man for our work."

"Very well, Camp," wrote Mr. Dexter, "employ him at once. Have you written to Rome?"

"Yes," replied Mr. Campion, "and Bangs has sailed to-day for Europe. I decided that it was best for him to go, as foreign interests, particularly of that nature, are more satisfactorily settled upon the spot. He will wire us and write full particulars as soon as he arrives in Rome. Do you wish

Nettie informed of her recent inheritance, or do you prefer to wait a while?"

"I shall improve now rapidly, I think," wrote Mr. Dexter; "so it will be better to wait until I am stronger before writing her anything about it. She will enjoy her visit better if she knows nothing. She is not one of the kind to rejoice at her own good fortune when she hears of her cousin's death or that her uncle is ill. I know her true, tender heart too well to inflict any sorrow upon her that can possibly be helped." Here Mr. Dexter was overcome by his feelings and the exertion of writing and lay back upon his pillow exhausted.

"I know; I know," said the attorney, sympathetically, after reading the message. "Nettie has a kind heart and an affectionate disposition. She is a dear, good girl and free from guile."

Then stating that he had much business to attend to, and tenderly pressing his friend's hand, he hastily took his departure. A few days after this interview Ferris, the Chicago detective, was in private conference with Augustus Campion in the inner office of Campion & Bangs, and the same evening he hastened to New York, where he began his search for Jim Bolan, *alias* Gentleman Jim, *alias* Antoinne DeLacey.

Ferris did not savor of the detective to the casual observer. He was not a person to attract attention, and would naturally pass for an ordinary business man. He was of medium height, and, when not disguised, had a round smooth face, with a light-colored moustache. His eyes were brown and wide open, as were his ears. The small, glittering black eyes, so commonly associated with the detective, were not his. One of his first acts was to visit the rogues' gallery, where he searched carefully among the pictures for one which might resemble that which he carried in his pocket of Bolan. He then inspected the prisoners in the jails of the city; unsuccessful here, he visited the hotels, copying off a long list of foreign names which had been registered at about the time when DeLacey would probably have arrived in America. Then began a long search in which he traced the course of some of these foreigners who had remained in New York City. He was very industrious, writing letters to all parts of the country, giving and asking information. He then visited and made personal investigations in Boston, Philadelphia, and Baltimore. He had photographs struck off and sent them to different correspondents. Once he thought he had found his man and hastened to Chicago, but his first glance at the person suspected told him that he was on the wrong track. During his stay in New York he stopped at a European hotel, much resorted to by sporting men and situated in the noisy part of the city, well down town. Here, oftentimes during his search, day and night, he would drop in and sit or stand about listening to the talk of the various frequenters of the place.

One night he returned to the hotel very late, and stepping into the bar-room, which led out of the office, to obtain a light for his cigar, he overheard the magic words "Gentleman Jim" pronounced in low tones by a man who was standing at the bar eagerly talking with a companion. Here perhaps was a clue. He was all attention, but as he passed them he appeared indifferent and unconscious; they immediately changed the subject, however, and in louder voices began discussing a horse-race which had occurred that day. Ferris, after lighting his cigar, strolled leisurely back into the hotel office, where, taking a seat which commanded a view of the bar-room entrance, he pretended to read a newspaper. After some delay the two men came out of the bar-room, and one of them stepping up to the clerk at the desk asked for the key to Room 186; then, as if undecided, consulted his companion a moment, and they both left the hotel, one of them casting a suspicious glance at the detective as they passed him. Ferris followed them carefully until he saw them enter a noted gambling-house. He then hastened back to the hotel and called for the proprietor.

"He is abed," said the clerk. "Anything particular?"

"Yes," said Ferris. "It is detective work."

"He won't get up for that, I'm afraid," said the clerk. "That's getting stale."

"My name is Ferris. I am from Chicago."

"Oh, yes," said the clerk. "I know. He'll get up for you."

Ferris explained to the landlord his suspicions, and they both went up to Room 186, which the landlord opened with a pass-key.

On entering the room they both noticed that the two men had their things all packed and ready, apparently, to move at a moment's notice. This aroused the landlord's suspicions. Something was wrong, and he immediately became more indulgent and agreeable. He told Ferris that the men had engaged the room for two weeks longer that very morning, telling him that they might want to stay a month. Ferris did not attempt to open or disturb the trunk and two valises which were in the room, as he did not wish to arouse their suspicions in any way. Upon the table he found some writing materials. One of the blotters he examined carefully and slipped it into his pocket; then seeing some bits of torn paper with writing upon them scattered about the floor, he, with the landlord's assistance, carefully picked up every piece, placing them also in his pocket. He remarked that there was a door connecting with the next room, number 184. This room, the landlord informed him, was unoccupied, and the door leading to it was bolted on both sides. He immediately engaged the room, and bidding the landlord good-night, he locked himself in Room 184. He then began to occupy himself in rather a singular manner. First he took the blotter out of his pocket and held it up before the mirror; after studying its reflection in the glass for a while, he was able to decipher a name and address. The name seemed to satisfy him, for with a smile he nodded his head two or three times knowingly, and then began working at the bits of paper, which he carefully spread out upon a table. He began matching the torn edges, and worked industriously until, after a long time, he succeeded in putting them all together nicely so that the words upon them made sense. The gray streaks of morning were beginning to light up the windows as he finished, and read with eager eyes the letter which had so strangely fallen into his hands.

Suddenly he heard movements in the next room. The men had evidently returned after an all-night struggle with fate at the gambling house.

Ferris pressed his ear closely against the crack of the door and listened carefully to hear what they might say to each other; but he was disappointed; they only grumbled a little at their losses at gambling and were soon in bed, and, as he knew by their hard breathing, fast asleep.

He then lit a cigar, sat down near the door connecting the two rooms, and patiently awaited their
awakening. This was a weary task. He heard
the clocks in the neighborhood strike hour after
hour and the growing hum of humanity inside and
out as the morning advanced.

Once he rang the bell and ordered some breakfast to his room; once he fell into a little doze
himself, from which he was startled by the striking
of a clock which indicated that it was noon, and
shortly after this he began to hear the occupants
of number 186 moving about. Again he placed his
ear to the door and listened. One of the men
finally spoke in a low tone to the other.

"'Ere's a go," said he, at once betraying his
nationality. " Blow me tight, but hi wouldent gif
a bob for luck ha roostin' 'ere hanother night.
We're the boys to be jugged sure's me name's
honest 'Arry."

" Whoy d'ye t'ink it?" said the other, who was
evidently Irish. The Englishman then went on to
say that he had noticed that they were followed
out of the hotel the night previous; he had dropped
his glove to get an opportunity to glance quickly
behind at Ferris. He didn't know who the " cove"
was, but he believed he was a spotter, and that
they were watched every minute. The Irishman
laughed at his fears, and, as if to prove that they
were not watched, suddenly opened the door lead-

ing into the hallway and looked out. The Englishman admitted that he was in no condition the night
before to cope with detectives and might be mistaken; he hoped he was, for they were comfortable
where they were and they must stay in New York
somewhere until Gentleman Jim obtained all of
the points about "the rich duffer's boodle."

"How the divil did Jim tumble on that lay?"
asked the Irishman, who evidently did not know
as much of Gentleman Jim's arrangements as
"honest 'Arry," who then proceeded in low tones
to tell the other how Bolan, on arriving in New
York, instead of going to a large hotel, had engaged expensive apartments at one of the more
secluded and aristocratic houses. Here he had
represented himself as an Englishman of wealth,
and had gradually formed the acquaintance of a
millionaire who made the same house his temporary home, but who resided a few miles out of New
York, where he owned a magnificent estate on the
Hudson. Bolan's plan was to induce him, if possible, to play high at cards, or, failing in this, to visit
his handsome residence by invitation, and while
there, help them "crack the crib," as he expressed
it. At present he said the millionaire was off
yachting on a summer cruise, and Bolan had gone
with him. Ferris carefully listened to everything
that was said until finally he heard them leave their
room and go away; then he made a memorandum

of it all, threw himself upon his bed, and was soon in a sound sleep.

He had not slumbered long, however, before he was aroused by a violent knocking at his room-door; opening it, he was confronted by two men who inquired if his name was Ferris. On reply-ing in the affirmative, they showed him detective badges and told him that they had orders from the chief of police to arrest two men on suspicion of implication in a daring robbery; that the landlord, who stood beside them, had informed them that the men who occupied number 186 were out. That they had instructions to bring all of the effects be-longing to the criminals to the central station, but that the landlord objected to their so doing until they had consulted him, as he (Ferris) was watch-ing the thieves. They had telephoned to head-quarters, and were instructed to see Ferris and get information concerning the men if possible.

Ferris told them that he knew nothing about the men, that he was working them to get at another party. Thanking him, they had the baggage from number 186 quickly transferred to a wagon and con-veyed away. They then took seats in the hotel office with Ferris, who had come down, to await the return of the two criminals. Ferris, thinking it unwise to be seen in company with two New York detectives should the thieves return, and feeling the need of nourishment, soon left them, and repaired to a restaurant near by for dinner. On his return the detectives had vanished. Suspecting something wrong, he at once telephoned to the chief of police at headquarters for information. The reply came that there were no such men on such a case; that they must be frauds. He then stepped into the bar-room and asked the bar-tender if he knew the two men who were in there a short time previous, describing them minutely.

" No, I don't know 'em," replied the dispenser of liquids. " But the feller wid a red top kep' a mill on the Bowery onct, in the Ole Felix House. I forgit his name, but he had a pard named Barney Magee, who runs a dive down on Pearl Street."

Ferris thanked him, and after changing his attire, disguised as a dissolute street loafer, he went in search of Barney Magee.

The reader may be curious to know how the bogus detectives knew about Ferris. The Irishman and his friend " honest 'Arry," after leaving the hotel, held a sort of council of war at a neighboring saloon, and decided that it was too dangerous to stay there longer. They then planned a method by which they could get away their baggage without paying their hotel bill, which was several weeks in arrears. They employed the help of two of their " pals" who were living in another part of the city, and who carried out the plan by acting as detectives, as we have seen. Walking boldly into the hotel, they asked to see the proprietor in private. In his private office they showed him their badges, and said they were after thieves who were occupying room number 186 in his hotel.

The landlord, remembering his experience of the night previous, was not surprised at this, but informed them that Ferris, the Chicago detective, was occupying number 184, and keeping watch over the thieves. The make-believe detectives pretended to know all about this, and offered to go up and interview Ferris and capture the thieves. Of course the birds had flown, and the bogus detectives took the baggage, as they had intended, placed it in a wagon which they had in waiting, and it soon disappeared in the busy whirl of the New York streets, as they did also soon afterward. Ferris had no difficulty in finding the establishment of Barney Magee; every policeman in that quarter of the city knew it intimately; in fact, he himself had been there on a previous visit to New York, and Magee had aided him in the capture of a noted Chicago criminal.

"*Dives*," strange as it may seem, only flourished by the tolerance and desire of the police authorities, because their proprietors were, in a measure, in the *secret-service* hire.

For a strange "*crook*" to enter one of them and make his headquarters was almost as certain detec-

tion and capture as would be an act of open robbery, with police for witnesses.

Ferris waited around in the neighboring saloons
until after dark, knowing that then he would be
more sure of finding Magee at home. At about
nine o'clock, however, he stumbled down the steep
stone steps of Magee's place, and into the bril-
liantly lighted room, pretending to be somewhat
ʳintoxicated. The apartment was foully laden with
the odor of poor tobacco and the fumes of stale
liquor. At various tables ranged along the sides
of the room sat brutal-looking men, who were trying to sap enjoyment out of cards, liquor, and vile
cigars. A weazen-looking Italian was painfully
twanging what he probably considered music upon
a badly-tuned and worse-toned harp, while standing by his side a dirty-looking overgrown urchin
was producing nerve-killing sounds from a violin.
Ferris, at a glance, took in all the occupants of the
room, staggered up to Magee, who was sitting,
like a king upon his throne, at a high desk on one
end of the bar.

But it is not our purpose to follow Ferris
through all of the disgusting details of his work
as a criminal detective. He was persistent in his
duty; was several times baffled, and many another
man would have become thoroughly discouraged;
but he always perseveringly surmounted difficulties, and without the slightest thought of aban-

doning his search. Often he was obliged to change his disguises; once he passed himself off as a thief from Boston, in order the more readily to enable him to enter the company and confidence of those he was watching; at another time he impersonated a country farmer, and allowed himself to be robbed by the very man whom he desired to get information from; finally, after about three weeks of continuous work, aided by the address which he had discovered upon the blotter at the hotel, he thought he possessed a clew which would enable him to find Gentleman Jim.

He wrote occasionally to Mr. Campion such matters as he considered of particular importance; but Ferris was not a man to make known his plans before he carried them out.

Thus time went on, and Mr. Dexter recovered sufficiently to sit up in a reclining chair. He still kept his illness a secret from Nettie, his niece, although he now wrote to her every week, detailing the home news as though nothing had happened to mar the usual serenity of his existence.

His physician held out to him such sanguine hopes of his ultimate recovery that he complied cheerfully with all directions, and devoted his whole time and mind to the recuperation of his health and strength.

CHAPTER X.

High Life on Deck—Van Dusen an Epicure—His Friends—A
Visit to Smoke Island—Craik Overdoes It—Alice Van Twist
as an Artist—Rescued from Drowning—The Paternal Parkins'
Pants—A Word for Physiognomy—Nettie sails " The Queen."

THERE was high living on board of the " Siren."
Van Dusen enjoyed his three or four kinds of
wine at dinner, and anticipated his cigar with
cognac and cordial. Not that he was a very in-
temperate man ; on the contrary, he was never
known to be unduly under the influence of liquor.
A large share of his life had been spent abroad.
Paris saw him the greater part of every other
winter, more because he enjoyed the customs of
the French than from any particular affection for
the French themselves. His weakness was French
cuisine. His French cook accompanied him upon
all of his yachting excursions ; and Mr. Van Dusen
never avoided trouble or expense to put himself
in possession of the dainties of the market. He
was one of those (shall we say fortunate ?) individuals who live to eat, but never dream as possible the reversal of such a proposition.
    Wine was to him what in a sense coffee is to

many, an established and habitual necessity; and
not having a gouty or apoplectic diathesis, and
possessing an enviable digestion and a most ami-
cable liver, he never stinted himself in any of these
luxuries of life.

But if Mr. Van Dusen was a man who so thoroughly enjoyed the eatables and drinkables of life,
he could not be accused of selfishness. He was a
model of generous hospitality. In fact, he was so
free-handed that it is safe to say he would not have
enjoyed his many pleasures alone. His guests,
too, upon the yacht, were appreciative. Professor
Romney was a man who had always been accustomed to luxury. Belonging to one of the
wealthiest families of his State, he had been reared
an epicure. Mr. Kendall was by nature æsthetic,
particularly fond of those things which brought
him gustatory satisfaction; while Craik was the
son (dissolute) of a wealthy clergyman of the
Episcopal faith, who for many years was as noted
for his fine table as for his lengthy but erudite
pulpit discourses.

In fact, their common liking for the luxuries of
the table was one of the main causes which had
thrown these four men together. Mentally, they
had little in common; physically, they were born
affinities. Van Dusen's mind had been nourished
in a moneyed soil. When the newspapers arrived
he devoted himself almost exclusively to the finan-

cial and commercial news; the professor selected
what was scientific, occasionally reading an edi-
torial; Mr. Kendall seldom read anything but a
sectarian organ, which was forwarded to him every
week with scrupulous punctuality; Craik was always eager to see the papers as soon as they arrived,
but seldom kept them long in his hands, and
seemed to skim them through as though searching for some expected piece of information.

Their bond of sympathy and good-fellowship
existed, therefore, by virtue of their good diges-
tions and fondness in indulging them. This was
the capital which held them together as a firm,
and thus far their enterprise seemed a successful
one. After the departure of Tom and his party,
they had voted Jack a clever fellow, the girls remarkably bright-minded and very handsome, while
Tom they spoke of differently. Mr. Van Dusen
said he was a good soul, but rather precocious;
Mr. Kendall said he thought he was intelligent, but
a slave to liberalism, which, if persisted in, would
in time ruin any good mind; Craik voted Tom a
fool, and did not hesitate to say so; while the professor grew red in the face as he sounded Tom's
praises in eulogistic language, which he ably commanded.

Early on the following morning three of the
yachting party took the yawl and started off for
an all-day fishing excursion, leaving Craik, who

said he wanted to rest, alone upon the yacht with two of the deck hands.

Craik did not seem to enjoy the life of a sportsman. His moments of real pleasure seemed to be when he was engaged at cards or over wine at dinner. Van Dusen was somewhat disappointed in him, for he had as yet discovered in him no true powers as a skilful conversationalist; and, outside of convivial matters, Craik had proved himself rather poor company for his guests. Therefore, when he refused to accompany them on their fishing excursion, Van Dusen was by no means disappointed, but rather satisfied.

The day had passed very slowly for Craik. He was restless and ill at ease. It was three o'clock as he lay snoozing under the deck-awning, his eyes occasionally glancing in the direction of Cup Island. Suddenly he saw the little boat shoot out from the island; two people were in it, and he correctly surmised that they were Miss Tillottson and her friend. They pulled directly for Smoke Island, where they landed and disappeared in the Van Twist cottage.

Craik, who was glad of an opportunity to see more of Belle, immediately took advantage of it. Getting quickly into the row-boat, and taking one of the sailors with him, he was pulled to Smoke Island, where, after landing and sending the man back with the boat, he walked leisurely up the

gentle slope toward the cottage. This visit of
Belle and Nettie to the Van Twist cottage was the
result of a courageous effort; it would have suited
their inclinations better to have taken one of their
exploring expeditions along the coast; but they
felt it a kind of duty to notice the only ladies in
the vicinity, and as Mrs. Tillottson, who was now
living with them upon Cup Island, had mildly
urged them to go, they finally made the effort.

The Van Twists received them very pleasantly.
Mother and daughter were sitting upon a little
portico or piazza upon one side of the cottage as
the girls arrived, where, after the usual greetings,
they all settled. The major was taking his afternoon nap. They were in the shadow, and could
enjoy the fine view of the water and the cool
breeze which was then blowing. Soon after their
arrival, Miss Van Twist, who had been describing
their bathing facilities to Belle, asked her to walk
to the beach and inspect their bathing-houses.
On their way down they met Mr. Craik.

Miss Van Twist greeted him very cordially,
telling him that she thought he was off upon a
fishing excursion, as she had seen the yawl start
in the morning; then, seeing no boat, she asked
him with some surprise how he had arrived.
Craik pointed with a smile to the boat which was
then just disappearing around a point of the island
in the direction of the yacht.

"I sent the man back to the vessel," he said, "where he has duties to perform. He will return for me if I signal."

"How very good of you to come over," said Miss Van Twist, smiling one of her most finished smiles. "It is so stupidly lonesome here sometimes."

"Impossible, in the company you now enjoy," said he, indicating by a glance that he meant Belle. "I have been alone upon the 'Siren' all day, and thought I would just run over for a moment to see if I could be of service to you in any way."

"It is very kind, I am sure," Miss Van Twist replied. "Miss Tillottson and I were on our way to the beach. Will you come with us and give us your opinion of our bathing-houses?"

"With pleasure," said Craik, glad of any chance which threw him in Belle's society.

They walked to the bathing-houses and sat upon the steps leading to the water below.

"Do you sketch, Miss Tillottson?" said Craik, after they had exhausted the subject of bathing.

"A little," Belle replied; "that is, I never have taken any instruction in drawing, but I amuse myself occasionally endeavoring to reproduce some of the odd scenes and sweet views which I see so often about here."

"Oh, I do think sketching is just delightful,"

said Miss Van Twist, who had devoted much time and money to it. " I have been crazy about it for years; I must show you both some of my drawings. I will run up to the house and get my sketch-book. Last year we were in the Alps, and I wish you to see one or two views which I think I succeeded in getting into my book quite successfully. Switzerland is too beautiful for anything."

" Except sketching," said Belle, with a smile.

" Let me get your book for you," said Craik.

" Oh, no indeed, thank you; I will go, for it is locked up in the bottom of my trunk; but I will soon return;" saying which Miss Van Twist hastened toward the cottage.

When she had disappeared, Craik, who had been somewhat serious up to this time, turned his handsome face toward Belle and said, cheerfully,—

" It is very beautiful here, Miss Tillottson, and it is hard to realize that such calm peacefulness cannot last forever. Beyond these placid waters men are rudely struggling with each other for supremacy in all things, for life itself and its necessities. Can it be possible that war, grim war, with all of its accompanying horrors, is now in progress in no less than five different nations of the earth? How serene is this sky, and what a supreme privilege that we, or more particularly I, should be allowed to peacefully sit here and drink in all of this intoxicating beauty. Will you pardon me if I congratulate you upon your delicacy of taste in wearing a costume so becoming, and at the same time so perfectly in harmony with these charming surroundings?"

The expression of Craik's face was so kindly that Belle could hardly take offence at his personal remarks, though she felt a natural shrinking from the man for taking what she considered an unwarrantable liberty, therefore, although somewhat provoked, she replied, gently,—

"Yes, life here is fascinating, extremely so; but the chief charm of the locality lies, I think, in its remarkable healthfulness."

While she was speaking Craik had unpinned from his coat a beautiful pink rose, which he had been wearing; and deftly throwing it into her lap, as she finished her remark, he said,—

"Pardon me, but there is an Oldport treasure which I am sure you cannot refuse, since you have so fairly won it by wearing a costume only lacking this flower to make it perfection."

Belle was passionately fond of pink roses; and although her inclination was to return him the flower, she, on second thoughts, decided that to accept it would be more ladylike, therefore she modestly thanked him and pinned the beautiful rose at her throat.

Craik was correct. With the rose Belle did

appear the perfection of loveliness. She wore a close-fitting gown of white material, a kind of flannel, cut and trimmed to show her beautiful figure to advantage. She had reluctantly arrayed herself in this costume to appear well before the Van Twists upon this her first visit to Smoke Island.

"Roses are by no means plentiful in this vicinity," said Belle, "and I am afraid that you are robbing yourself by your generosity; but you are so reckless with the dear flower that I feel in duty bound to act as its zealous protector."

"It could not possibly have a more charming defender," said Craik, sitting a little closer to Belle; then noticing her embarrassment and rising indignation, he added, quickly, "but I was aware of this before parting with it, so you can hardly maintain the charge of recklessness. Do see that sea-gull, Miss Tillottson, he has captured a fish, almost too heavy for him to carry. What will he do?"

Belle had arisen and was making a motion to return to the cottage when Alice Van Twist arrived accompanied by Nettie.

"Oh, you were just about to come after me, were you?" she said, as if in half apology for her absence. "I was unable to unlock my trunk easily. Well, we will all return together as soon as we have shown Miss Knowles the bathing-houses."

Presently, therefore, they strolled back to the cottage, Craik placing himself at Belle's side.

"I hope I did not offend you by my remarks a few moments ago," he said, in a low, penitent voice, as they walked along. "I spoke impulsively. Thoughts find words sometimes in spite of us. There are times when one grasps at a friendship as a drowning man seizes a straw. My life has been far from a happy one, Miss Tillottson. May I say that a fair knowledge of human nature leads me to hope that you will be my friend?"

"I am sure I have no desire to be an enemy to any one," said Belle, scarcely realizing what she said.

"I knew that you would not hate me without true cause," said he; "and yet I feel that I have been indiscreet; but, with the knowledge of your forgiveness and the assurance of your friendship, I can never regret that my indiscretion has brought about such happy results."

By this time they had reached the cottage, and Belle, with an inward sigh of relief, attached herself to Mrs. Van Twist.

Craik's last remarks had by no means added to her composure. What right had he, an almost total stranger, to assume that she would be his friend or that he had her forgiveness? Indeed, she was not his friend, and would never forgive him. Had he been truly a gentleman he would

have passed over the incident of the rose, never
referring to it again. She could not understand
why, on such a brief acquaintance, he should dare
to assume an air of familiarity. Jack *never* would
have done such a thing, although Jack had given
her many flowers. Jack was very kind; but pre-
sumptuous, *never*. She wished Jack could know
how intensely she disliked this Mr. Craik. Perhaps Mr. Craik would now seize every favorable
opportunity to appear familiar when Jack was present; if he dared do such a mean thing she would
surely be rude toward him. She had a good mind
to tell Jack all about it. Thus her thoughts flew;
and she felt tears gathering in her eyes, her throat
was uncomfortable, and she wondered if her face
was not red. Pshaw! What was Jack Stratton to
her? Well, he was her friend, at least; and she
smiled involuntarily as she thought to herself that
Jack did like her very much. As for Craik, if he
was awfully handsome, he was not her friend.
How did he dare assume that such was the
case? She would tell Nettie all about it, and ask
her advice.

Now, all of this time Belle was carrying on a
desultory conversation with Mrs. Van Twist. The
latter, in her characteristic way, had been making
some inquiries of her in regard to the quality,
methods of construction, and place of purchase
of her gown,—the impertinence of which inquiries

Belle entirely overlooked in her excitement, good-naturedly vouchsafing all of the desired information.

The sketch-book was passed around and more than duly admired. Who dares to criticise the labored productions of an amateur, especially when the artist is a young woman? They were drawings possessing some merit for accuracy of outline and perspective, evidently hard-won virtues, but they lacked that naturalness of expression which is given by a master of *chiaroscuro*. They were also wanting in the boldness of style which indicates true talent. There was nothing of Cruikshank or Doré boldness about them : every stroke of the pencil, *and there were many*, was made as though the designer had a doubt as to its right of place; and this hesitancy in particulars gave to the grand total an appearance of mediocrity, reflecting seriously upon the skill of the sketcher.

While they were occupied with these drawings, Jack and the doctor, who had been sent over by Mrs. Tillottson to bring home the girls, arrived upon Smoke Island. The young men were somewhat surprised to find Craik there, but politely offered to take him back to the "Siren" in "The Queen"; which offer, although urged by the Van Twists to stay to tea, he readily accepted. The Van Twists were also profuse in their invitations to the young people, urging them to come over often, the major joining his wife and daughter in these overtures. He had a look of sleepiness upon his red face as he appeared upon the porch, and cordially joined in the conversation.

He said if they would stay to tea he would give them some fish of his own catching, and that ought to be a great inducement; but they politely declined the invitations, and reminding the Van Twists that they were all to meet on the morrow on board of the " Siren," they took their departure, and were soon sailing away for the Van Dusen yacht.

On " The Queen," Craik, as Belle had feared, was obsequious in his attentions. His hand it was which anticipated Jack's in helping her on board, and he hastily, almost rudely, took measures to insure himself a seat by her side; while he kept up a running conversation during their short sail to the " Siren."

" Are you ever sea-sick, Miss Tillottson ?" he asked, as soon as they were under way.

" I never have been," replied Belle, civilly.

" Nor I," said Craik; " but so many people are that I sometimes feel, when at sea, as though it were almost my duty to be so. Probably, if I once tried it, I should be effectually cured of any such notion. A certain friend of mine, in crossing the Atlantic, never deserts his state-room from the time he leaves America until he reaches Ireland, where he is glad of an opportunity to land at Queenstown and take a week or so to recuperate before crossing St. George's Channel. It is amusing to watch the passengers on board an ocean steamer as soon as the sea begins to get a little rough. They are generally well stocked with remedies, which their friends have recommended as sure preventives of sea-sickness. I remember once meeting an old lady who was enthusiastic in her recommendation of hot water. A glass of hot water whenever one began to feel dizzy, she said, acted like a charm to drive away that bugbear of the ocean traveller. Since then, I believe that hot-water advocates have become quite numerous. I would not mind having a little touch of the complaint, just to test the efficacy of that old lady's prescription. She charged me particularly to be careful not to have the water too cool, as water which was simply lukewarm might prove disastrous."

Belle could not repress a wee smile.

" Have you ever taken an ocean voyage?" he said, encouraged to continue his exertions to please.

" I never have crossed the ocean; but I once sailed from New York to Savannah, and was the only lady out of over fifty who did not miss a meal during the trip. The captain said I was a good sailor."

" And so you would be," said Craik, delighted

at this little effort on Belle's part to keep up the conversation. "It is certainly very tiresome, not to say discouraging, to start with a party on a voyage, and before you have been a whole day upon the ocean have them disappear, one by one, into their state-rooms, leaving you alone to enjoy yourself as you can."

At this juncture Tom, who had the helm, was obliged, or thought it best, to put about, and requested them to change their seats. In doing this Jack, who was on the lookout for just such a manœuvre, managed to quietly slip down alongside of Belle, leaving Craik to sit alone.

This movement amused Jack immensely, and put him quickly in good spirits.

"Boots," said Tom, gayly, "what do you suppose Jack and I have been doing all day?"

"You can have three good square guesses," said Jack; "and if you hit upon the right thing I will forfeit a box of caramels, which, by the way, are to be had almost instanter, or as soon as we arrive upon the hospitable shores of Cup Island."

"Breathing!" said Belle, delighted to get beside Jack again, and responding to his gayety in like mood. "There! I have fairly won the caramels,—haven't I, Nettie?"

"Yes," said Nettie, clapping her hands. "That was a true guess, and I don't see how he can get around it."

"Well," said Jack, pretending to be crestfallen, "trust a woman to edge her way out of a difficulty. When I get into trouble I shall know where to apply for a first-class pilot. The caramels are yours sure enough, Miss Tillottson, but Tom and I have been doing something besides breathing."

"Yes," said Tom, eager to tell their experience. "We started this morning for the long shoals, just south of the Millville light-house, expecting to have a good day at fishing; but, when opposite the point, we saw a row-boat just ahead of us capsize, throwing two children—a boy and a girl—into the water. I headed 'The Queen' for them at once, and in a twinkling we were alongside, when I rounded her up to the wind and brought her to a dead standstill. The sail flapped so for a moment that I could see nothing; but I heard a splash, and as soon as I could see, there was Jack close alongside buffeting the waves with one arm and holding the little girl in the other. I threw him the painter and soon had them both on deck."

"But the boy!" said both of the girls, excitedly. "What became of the boy?"

"Oh, he could swim," said Tom. "He was sitting on top of the upturned boat and we yanked him aboard in a jiffy, looking like a drowned rat; but Jack saved the little girl, and she is a perfect little beauty, by the way."

"Well," said Jack, with a comical look upon his

handsome face, " we took the youngsters ashore
and found that they were the children of the man
who keeps the Millville light-house, who in agony
had witnessed the catastrophe from the beach."

" Call it rather a fortunate rescue," said Belle.

" He was a pleasant man, and invited us up to
his house, where we have been for the greater part
of the day playing the part of forlorn shipwrecked
sailors."

" He was a delightful old party, I can assure
you.   Boots, you must sketch his jolly weather-
beaten face," said Tom.

" He showed us the great light which is his constant care," said Jack, " made us stay to dinner
although we had lunch with us, and it seemed as
though the old fellow could not do enough for us."

" His wife, too," said Tom, " was as kind and as
attentive as himself, so, altogether, we had a very
pleasant day, and left them at last after promising
that we would return, and bring all of our friends."

" You must have been uncomfortably wet," said
Belle to Jack.

" Yes," said Tom.   " Boots, if you could have
seen Jack rigged out in the duds of that old salt
you would have laughed.   The old chap is only
about five feet high, and as round as a barrel ; why,
he must weigh over two hundred."

" Yes," said Jack, his eyes twinkling with fun.
" I have a picture of myself in my mind's eye.

Captain Parkins—that was his name—loaned me his Sunday habiliments, and his wife kindly hung up my clothes to dry before the kitchen fire. The pants were airy, and only reached to my knees; with a little gathering they might have passed for the correct thing in knickerbockers. By the way, Doc, did you ever eat such huckleberry-pie as that which Mrs. Parkins set before us? It was delicious."

"So it was," said Tom, smacking his lips.

By this time they had reached the "Siren," where they parted with Mr. Craik, who had not said much since his separation from Belle. They remained only long enough to give Craik a chance to step on board of the yacht; and as they turned to sail away Van Dusen, who had been sitting on deck with his friends, reminded them of their prospective ocean sail on the morrow; and stepping to the side of the "Siren" requested them to be sure to come aboard as early as nine in the morning, as they wanted to take advantage of the tide-favor.

"Well, young ladies," said Tom, as soon as they were out of hearing, "is the dreadful ice broken at last, and were the Van Twists cordial?"

"Yes, indeed," Nettie replied; "but we saw little of them alone, for Mr. Craik arrived shortly after we did. He tried to make himself very agreeable, —didn't he, Belle?"

"I think the Van Twists are rather lonely there

on Smoke Island, and are glad to be relieved occasionally by a little company," said Belle, avoiding an answer to Nettie's question about Craik.

But for some reason Nettie did not use her usual good judgment, and again asked, perhaps with a little shrewd intention, though not provokingly,—

"You had an excellent opportunity to cultivate a friendship with Mr. Craik, I noticed. Is he not very entertaining?"

Jack's ears were wide open, and Belle thought she noticed that he was not pleased at what Nettie had intimated, while Tom looked anxiously at her.

"Mr. Craik," said Belle, desperately, "tried to make himself agreeable. He has some ways which appear rather strange to me, but perhaps he has acquired them abroad."

It was not Belle's intention to expose Mr. Craik's rudeness to the young men. She knew too well their indignation would know no bounds, and probably take a form of resentment which would result in violence, and she wished to avoid all discord during their stay upon Cup Island. She had made up her mind to tell Nettie all about Craik's strange language and behavior when they were alone, therefore she gave her one of those looks, the interpretation of which is known only to women, and effectually silenced her upon the subject of Craik during the rest of the sail.

Craik was provoked with himself for having been so precipitate. Why, thought he to himself, did I not put a curb upon my devilish tongue? He was angry with himself that he should have allowed his feelings to so master his reason and good judgment. He was delighted, however, at the prospect of seeing Belle again in the morning, and amused himself by planning various ways of amusing her when they should meet.

Craik was the son of an American clergyman. He had been brought up in a most refined circle, had received a liberal education, graduating from one of the leading colleges; but he early evinced a strong taste for low company and for the gaming-table. This latter taste led him to procure funds by dishonest methods. He confiscated and sold for a pittance the little valuables about his father's house, such as his mother's jewelry, the family plate, and his father's valuable books; these he would pawn or sell at a ridiculous discount upon their actual worth.

Thus matters went with him from bad to worse until one day he was arrested for theft, and the evidence being conclusive against him, he was sent to jail.

As there were no extenuating circumstances connected with this last act, it was a blow to his injured father's pride which he could not endure, and shortly after this evidences of the boy's otherwise dastardly conduct coming to the father's ears, Craik was denounced before the world, and they were separated forever. This action on the part of the reverend gentleman was not wholly unexpected by people who knew Craik. It came after many and repeated offences; numerous sins which had brought disgrace to the family had been condoned in the vain hope that some day the son would change his habits, as he had so often promised to do. In vain had the loving father pleaded with and appealed to the better nature of the boy, sometimes using strong measures to restrain his wicked tastes. What more could he do? The son was at times repentant, promising with tears in his eyes to amend his evil ways. Alas! for the poor parents; even the mother's tender love, gentle persuasiveness, and willing forgiveness were lost upon this child of Satan, and he wandered away from home an outcast and a fugitive from justice. For some years he roamed about the Western country associating with a miserable class of beings, with whom his tastes were congenial; later he drifted over to England, where his career became notorious, and his boldness, aided by his beauty of face and manner, enabled him to profitably carry out his vicious schemes. He was the more dangerous because possessed of those physical gifts which win their way so irresistibly among average mankind. The world is fortunate not to harbor many such men; and if people were better physiognomists they could not flourish at all.

Jack did not admire Craik. He saw the cruel line of his mouth when at rest, which the thick black moustache failed to entirely conceal. This mouth-line formed an oval opening, slightly exposing his front teeth near the median line. He saw the tendency to straight lines of the lower eyelids, and the deceptive look in the outer corners of the eyes. He saw also the want of definiteness in the contour lines about the chin and the lack of frontal development in the otherwise well-rounded cranium; all of which indications of his true character would not be noticed by the casual observer. Physiognomy is as yet an almost unknown science. People are judged now more by what they say and do than by their physical characteristics. Of course, to the uninitiated this is the safest method, but not always the surest. It is difficult to become so familiar with the complex lines of human nature that a character may be read by them at sight. In following the fascinating study of physiognomy, obstacles and complications meet the student at every step, making advance in knowledge more and more difficult. The vocabulary of the science is unlimited; types even have but an approximate definiteness, and the same infinite variety may be traced in the features of man that we meet in the multitudinous forms of nature. This fact, however, should not discourage the beginner. The infinite stares at us in any line of study in which nature is a factor. The fact that no two trees, nay leaves, are alike argues not that we should renounce botany; the multifarious varieties and species in the animal kingdom do not render zoology useless; and for the same reasons physiognomy, although an occult and complex study, should not be relegated to the ranks of useless research, nor considered in any sense an obsolete science. In fact, it is quite the reverse. Did we but realize it, we might be able to understand how intimately it is connected with the study of God. Surely as man is monarch of the created universe, so physiognomy or the study of physical man should take the leading place in that king of studies, physico-theology. By and through the phenomena of the natural world alone are we, as far as we are capable of knowing, enabled to form our conceptions of the true nature of God. We are told that we are made in His image and likeness; granting this, how can we more clearly arrive at a satisfying realization of His greatness and goodness than by familiarizing ourselves with the human economy? Although at present in the swaddling clothes of investigation, we are steadily working our way up to a proper knowledge of man by unravelling the mysteries of nature. Geology, botany, zoology, and physics are the stepping-stones toward the treasure-house in which lie hidden the *arcana* of human greatness; but the. mysteries which veil the great Unknown can only be revealed by a careful and persevering study of man himself. A man's face is a reflection of his soul, and reflex action stamps the external with a likeness of the internal man. More men know this than will acknowledge it, yet they unconsciously admit it by striving to wear a facial mask to hide their true character. It is the delight of the enthusiastic student of physiognomy to penetrate these masks, exposing the true man beneath. This faculty is uncommon, but is oftenest found among professional men. Physicians are made the confidants of humanity, and thus have uncommon facilities for comparing notes in the study of physiognomy.

The proverbial intuitive perception of woman is due, no doubt, in a great measure, to her ability as a natural physiognomist.

Artists or portrait-painters are generally good judges of character, because they make a particular study of features. Thus by long practice and experience they have connected certain types of character with their corresponding outlines of features. The caricaturist is in some degree a natural physiognomist. He illustrates the striking or prominent characteristics of a face by exaggerating those features which he believes represent them.

Jack, as we have before stated, had this peculiar power. His opinion of Craik was unfavorable, and, besides, it disturbed him greatly that he should have paid Miss Tillottson so much marked attention.

He did not believe that Belle liked the man; but it interfered with the peace of his mind that she should be bothered by such a person, and he resolved that in future, if it were in his power, he would prevent it. He was therefore quite silent and thoughtful during the short sail homeward, and Belle, who noticed this, felt that she could guess the reason.

Tom gave Nettie the tiller, and, standing near, instructed her in the management of the boat; while she, following his directions to the letter, proved herself capable of some day becoming an efficient sailor by guiding " The Queen" safely over the placid waters of the harbor and rounding her up neatly at the little pier at Cup Island, where Mrs. Tillottson stood awaiting their arrival with a motherly smile upon her handsome face.

CHAPTER XI.

Nettie's Letter to her Uncle—A few Lines from Jonathan Ferris—
Is Mr. Craik Jim Bolan?—Comparing Pictures—Uncle Camp
decides to go to Oldport—A Letter from Mr. Bangs—Nettie an
Heiress.

ADAM DEXTER, as we have seen, was a man
capable of strong emotions, a man of powerful
feelings. It had always been a struggle with him
to substitute good judgment and cool decisive-
ness for inclination. He longed during the first
part of his illness for the affectionate care and
loving presence of his niece, and his impulse was
to send for her at once, but his better nature con-
quered, and, as we know, he kept her in total
ignorance of his misfortune. Now, therefore, as
he sat on a beautiful August morning near the
open window, and felt the glow of health returning to his pallid cheeks, his heart filled with
gratitude at the thought of what he had saved his
dear Nettie. He knew that she would be somewhat grieved when she was informed of Roger's
death; but she was so young when the boy left
home that her grief would be more from her concern for his own sorrow than for the loss of her
almost forgotten cousin. He was doubly anxious,

therefore, to appear as well as possible when she returned home, and to this end he now devoted his entire mind and activities. He desired, there-fore, to postpone her return for the present, or until he should be greatly improved in health.

He had just received and read a letter from Nettie, in which she had given a graphic description of their yachting trip upon the " Siren ;" and it was over this letter that Mr. Dexter sat ruminating and listening to the songs of the birds as their blithesome notes were wafted in through the open windows by the balmy midsummer breezes, when a servant entered and announced his lawyer and friend, Mr. Campion.

"Well, well," said the attorney, shaking him cordially by the hand; "it is jolly to find you sitting up in such fine feathers and looking so hearty. Why, you will be a better man than I am in six weeks. Bless my soul, you are a marvel, indeed, to recuperate so rapidly."

"Yes," said Mr. Dexter, slowly, for he could now enunciate though not without some effort, "I am getting stronger. I have taken quite a little walk this morning up and down the room here; and I feel that horrible prickly numbness slowly leaving me; for which I am truly thankful. Any news this morning, Camp?"

"Nothing of any importance, I fear," he replied. "Ferris writes me that he is slowly but surely getting nearer his man; but I brought you his letter, which you can read for yourself if you wish."

"Yes," said Mr. Dexter, eagerly, "let me have it; and here is a letter from Nettie which I know you will be pleased to read while I am going over this. There is a message in that for you too."

"Yes, indeed," said the lawyer, taking Nettie's letter and passing the one from Ferris; "I am always glad to hear from the little witch. Hello, she is still at Cup Island with the Tillottsons. Nice people those Tillottsons. I knew the father, Thomas Tillottson, well in my younger days. We were at college together, and always kept up a sort of intimacy afterward."

Mr. Dexter ran his eyes over the following:

"MESSRS. CAMPION & BANGS:

"*Gentlemen,*—There is not much for me to write this week except that I am correct in thinking that I have a clew to my man. He is at present planning to rob a man of wealth with whom he is now on a yachting trip. Who this wealthy gentleman is I have not yet discovered, but I know that he first met him at some hotel in this city, and I think that I can soon get his name; but I must first bag the confederates in the scheme, who are at present awaiting Bolan's return to New York.

I am on their track, and have possession of a letter which they thought destroyed implicating them in the great Chicago robbery. I have also the address of a co-operator of theirs in Chicago, whom I know well, and for whose capture the authorities have offered a large reward. By the time you receive this I shall have this man in limbo, as I start for Chicago in half an hour. If we can induce this rogue to turn state's evidence,—and I think we can when I whisper certain facts in his ear,—he may give us the present hiding-place of the rest of the gang, who are, I think, somewhere in the Eastern States. I can through them probably get at Gentleman Jim. There are so many yachts in and around New York, and they change location and ownership so often, that it would be very slow work getting him in that way, and I do not advise it; therefore I have decided to adopt the other course, and kill two birds (or perhaps half a dozen) with one stone.

"Send information as usual to headquarters in Chicago for a week or two.

"Yours truly,

"JONATHAN FERRIS."

During Mr. Dexter's perusal of this letter the lawyer was plodding with a half-amused smile and an occasional laugh through the following from Nettie:

"CUP ISLAND, August —, 18—.

"MY OWN PRECIOUS UNCLE,—Just think! it is a whole week since I have written to you. It is too bad, and I am real sorry, but I have been so much occupied, and there are so many things to do here, that it is difficult to find opportunity to write. I can never rely upon being uninterrupted for five minutes. Even now, as I write, Belle, her brother, and Mr. Stratton are singing a lovely trio downstairs, and I am tempted to rush down and join them in their song. I am so glad, dear uncle, that I came here with Belle and her mother. Dr. Tillottson is so kind, and is such a splendid man to have on such an expedition, that it would be hard to get along without him. He knows how to do almost everything, and his friend, whom he calls 'Jack,' keeps us laughing nearly all the time with his jokes and oddities. I never felt so well and strong in all my life, and am getting so stout that I am afraid of extravagant dressmakers' bills in the fall. Sometimes I feel much as though you needed me with you; you must be so dreadfully lonesome. Now, if you do need me, I will come home at once, for I could not be happy here if I thought you were not comfortable. I began to tell you in my last letter about our yachting trip with Mr. Van Dusen, but was interrupted. An ocean sail he called it. His yacht is called the 'Siren,' and is furnished magnificently.

"Mr. Stratton says that Mr. Van Dusen is a millionaire. I should certainly think so from his luxurious way of living. His three friends are nice,—that is, two of them are: Professor Romney, who is an intensely interesting conversationalist, and Mr. Kendall, a clergyman, who is a very earnest man. The other is a Mr. Craik. His claims to distinction seem to lie solely in his beauty of person. He is the finnicky pink of perfection in manner and appearance; but we none of us like him very well.

"Mr. Stratton drew a picture of him, a sort of caricature, which is so good that I enclose it for you to see. Mr. Craik is very dark, almost like a Spaniard, and extremely good-looking; but his tastes do not seem to harmonize with ours, and he is restless and preoccupied, and at all times ill at ease about something.

"I think he has fallen in love with Belle. Poor Belle, it is just her luck. You remember how it was at home last winter. Mr. Craik sends her beautiful flowers almost every day and comes here to Cup Island nearly every evening.

"Belle dislikes him, but, not wishing to be rude, treats him civilly. He has been abroad a great deal, and seems familiar with French and Italian life. I think from his speech that he has been much in England. The day we went yachting we sailed over fifty miles, and went ashore at a place

p

on the end of Long Island called Oyster Point.
We built a large bonfire upon the beach in which
we roasted oysters, clams, fish, and green corn.
Oh, uncle, they did taste so good! Then after
hunting for shells and sea-mosses for awhile we
went on board the 'Siren' again and sailed out
upon the ocean. It was lovely until it began to
get so rough that I was afraid Belle would be sea-
sick. Mrs. Tillottson and her sister went with us,
and I never saw anybody enjoy anything as she
did that sail. She is improving so much in health
and appearance that it is a delight to see her. Her
sister, Miss Tremane, or Aunt Deborah, as Belle
calls her, is too funny for anything, not a bit like
Mrs. Tillottson. She is what we call countryfied;
but she is awfully funny. I must tell you something she said to me to-day which made me laugh.
She was speaking of her health here by the sea,—

"'Oh, I'm right peart 'nuff'—that's the way she
talks—'so fur as health goes,' said she, 'if I could
only walk spruce. Yer see, I've a bunion on me left
foot and the rheumatiz in me right hip, so I don't
git around as lively as a cricket; but, thank goodness, I don't limp, for the bunion balances the
rheumatiz and the rheumatiz balances the bunion,
so I'm glad I've got 'em both at the same time.'

"Mr. Craik was very attentive to Belle during
the sail, and I was much amused watching them,
for you see Jack (that is what we all call Mr.

Stratton) has been perfectly devoted to Belle ever
since we have been here, and I know that she
likes him immensely; so Mr. Craik's attentions
were somewhat ill-timed. Of course, Jack and
Mr. Craik were brought much together with Belle,
and it was very funny. I felt real sorry for Jack,
who seems to be such a good-hearted fellow, and
the soul of honor. I am afraid that Belle did not
enjoy herself very well, although she insists that
she had a delightful time. I am sure I did.

"Why, uncle darling, I actually learned how to
sail the yacht. Mr. Van Dusen allowed me to
take the wheel, and he and Dr. Tillottson, who
manages a boat splendidly, kindly gave me lessons
in navigation. This was on our way home, and it
is too funny for anything what happened. I had
been steering the 'Siren' for perhaps twenty minutes, obeying instructions to the letter, when all
of a sudden there was not a breath of wind; we
were in a dead calm. Of course, we did not budge
an inch for over an hour, and thus ingloriously
ended my first real experience as a skipper. You
must know, dear uncle, that skipper means captain.

"The sun poured down upon us, but we were
all very jolly, and the gentlemen pretended that
they could raise a breeze by whistling. They
whistled and whistled, but not a puff of wind
came to our poor loose sails, except what they
produced from their lungs. We had our supper

on board of the yacht, and were all as hungry as wolves. There are a hundred things that I would like to write about to-day, but they are beginning to call me from below, and are getting impatient for me to join them, so I will be obliged to close this rambling sort of chat. I shall have all the more to tell though if I don't write about everything now. Rest assured that I am very, very happy, and perfectly well, as my enormous appetite will amply testify; and I am, dear uncle, just the same as ever, with an old-fashioned hug and kiss,

"Your bouncing big girl,

"NETTIE."

"P.S.—Please tell Susan not to forget to give 'Dickie' his chickweed, and I hope she gives him his bath every morning during this hot weather. I am glad he sings so beautifully and has finished moulting. I carry your letters about with me, uncle dear, and read them over and over again. It is so good of you to write all of the news.

"Give my love to dear Uncle Camp, and all who ask after me.   N."

Mr. Campion, after reading carefully every word of the letter, turned quickly to his friend, and asked for the drawing of Craik which had been enclosed. Mr. Dexter said he had not seen it, but after a little search among the papers upon his table he found it.

The lawyer examined it carefully, and producing a photograph from his pocket compared the two.

" Just as I suspected," said he, " when I began to read Nettie's letter. I believe that this Mr. Craik and James Bolan or Gentleman Jim, *alias* Antoinne DeLacy, *alias* Peter Worden, son of the Reverend Elias Worden, are one and the same person.

" The pictures, though very different in some respects, are nevertheless strikingly alike. Here in the photograph he has long hair and a full beard, while in the drawing he has on a broad-brimmed hat, his beard is shaved, and his hair is cut short; but the resemblance is striking, particularly about the eyes."

Mr. Dexter took the pictures, and, after examining them carefully, said that he could see no resemblance between them whatever; that the pencil drawing represented a much younger man than the photograph.

" Well, I think that they both represent one and the same individual," said the lawyer; " at any rate, if you will permit me, I will send the drawing to Ferris. He has one of the photographs in his possession. He can judge better than we."

" Certainly, by all means," said Mr. Dexter. " The clew is a faint one, but, after all, it may be good. The man is certainly on a yacht and with a millionaire."

"Yes," said Mr. Campion; "and I believe we have discovered our man in this Craik. Now if the yachting party only stay where they are long enough, we will soon be able to have him in custody. Ferris will jump at this clew, and as soon as he can finish his Chicago business will probably think best to go to Oldport at once."

"If this man Craik is such a rascal," said Mr. Dexter, very seriously, "I don't like the idea of his being so near my Nettie. I shall be much troubled until I know that he is attended to."

"I have been thinking of that, too," said the lawyer, quickly. "I'll tell you what I think had best be done, Dexter."

"Well, what is it?"

"I think," said Mr. Campion, "that I had better go to the dear child at once, or in a few days. My legal business is not driving me at present, and Sniffen can easily attend to whatever turns up during my absence; besides, I need a sniff of salt air myself, and a few weeks more or less at the sea-shore will do me a power of good. I am acquainted, you know, with Mrs. Tillottson; her husband was a noble soul. I remember once I went with him in November, some years ago, for a week or ten days, duck-shooting, on this very Cup Island, as he called it, where he had a cosey little

cottage. It was fine sport, and the air there was
marvellously invigorating. I know I shall greatly
enjoy a trip there again. I can find some boarding-place at Oldport, you know, and I can keep
Nettie in sight most of the time and watch Craik
for Ferris. I don't want Ferris to hurry away
from Chicago until he has captured those rascals
there."

"My dear Camp," said Mr. Dexter, "your offer
is generous and characteristic; but are you quite
certain that out of the kindness of your heart you
are not offering to do this greatly against your
own best interests? Will you not be putting yourself to great inconvenience by thus leaving your
affairs in the hands of a clerk, especially when
Bangs is away?"

"Oh, Sniffen is all right," said Campion: "he
has been with us so long that we place the most
implicit confidence in him; and as for my action
being generous, that's all nonsense, Dexter. I
must go somewhere this summer. You don't
want a fellow to work himself to death, do you?
I shall go; and I shall have a jolly good time, for
I love that little lass of yours almost as though
she were my own child."

"Well, if you are determined to go, and feel that
it will be a pleasure to you, Camp, I am sure I
think it an excellent plan," said Mr. Dexter, who
was inwardly delighted to have his stalwart friend

volunteer as Nettie's protector; "but I do not wish Nettie to know of my illness, or of Roger's death, just yet. She would immediately come home to me, and it would make the dear child very miserable to see me in this condition."

"She shall know nothing about it, if I can prevent it," said the lawyer, decisively, "until you have a few more weeks to recuperate."

"My physician says that I may be strong enough to walk in the garden next week," said Mr. Dexter; "and he advises me to drive out by the last of this week, and if there are no bad effects from it to drive after that as often and as much as I desire."

"That is good news, indeed, my dear fellow," said the lawyer, joyfully, making a merry pretence of slapping his invalid friend upon the back, while the glittering evidences of sympathetic weakness hung suspended for a moment in the corners of his eyes.

"Perhaps you had better write Nettie a line telling her that I am coming, and will be there on,— let me see,—well, say Thursday; that will give me three days to get my affairs into good shape here. My daughter, Josie, is with my brother's family at Long Branch, where she will remain for the present."

Augustus Campion was not a man to do things by halves. After leaving his friend he began immediately to make his preparations for departure.

Entering his office he informed Sniffen, the clerk, of his intention, and forthwith began to instruct him in those details which would need attention during his absence, carefully making notes of everything with his usual system. His mail was to be forwarded to the Oldport post-office, and Sniffen was to keep him informed daily by letter or, if necessary, by wire, of those important business events which might transpire. The adjustment of his office and other business was by no means a small undertaking for a man with so many irons in the fire, and naturally it took him several days to accomplish it; but he kept perseveringly at work, not omitting the smallest item, and at last felt that he could comfortably leave for a few weeks, or even longer, if necessary. The day before his departure he received a letter from Mr. Bangs, his partner, written at Rome, which read as follows:

"ROME, ITALY, July —, 18—.

"MY DEAR CAMPION,—I have arrived here but a few hours since, but have already seen the legal representatives of the deceased, and also have interviewed Mr. Moses Wigand, the partner of aforesaid. To be brief, I find the estate standing about as follows:

"A one-third interest in banking firm, which is represented by stock and other collateral, and which will have to be settled by sale of joint securities and withdrawal of such capital. Roger Dexter, or, as he was known here, Dexter Rogers, was also the owner of a handsome villa, at present closed up. It is situated in the outskirts of Rome. This property is rapidly increasing in value, and, being very desirable, can be easily turned into cash, should I get your instructions to that effect. The balance of the estate consists of personal property, in the shape of government, railroad, and manufacturing securities, which, of course, I will investigate and keep in the most desirable shape. I enclose detailed list with affidavit. . . .

"I feel tip top. This Italian air is fine. Rome has changed but little since you and I were here together.

"Wigand is a fine man. He was very much attached to Roger, says he loved him as a brother. Have written to Sarah, my wife, by same mail. Please drop around to the house as soon as convenient, and see that she and the children are all right. Will write again in a day or two. In regard to the villa, it would seem to me wise to hold it for a rise, particularly as it will always bring an excellent rent.

"In haste, yours,

"BANGS."

Mr. Campion hastened with this letter to Mr. Dexter, stopping at the residence of Mr. Bangs on the way to see Mrs. Bangs and have a few cheering words with the children.

"Now," said the lawyer to Mr. Dexter, after the latter had carefully read Mr. Bangs's letter, "what had we better do about the villa? Bangs writes that it is a good investment."

"Well," said Mr. Dexter, "what do you think?"

"A great deal depends upon what would be Nettie's desire in the matter," replied Mr. Campion.

"I don't think she would care much one way or the other," Mr. Dexter replied. "If she married she might choose to enjoy a winter there occasionally, and her ample means would warrant such an enjoyment; if she continued single, however, she would not have much use for a Roman villa."

"I am inclined to think," said Mr. Campion, "that we had better act for Nettie just the same as we would for ourselves. If the property is an excellent investment, and, as Bangs writes, will bring a profitable income, it might be the wisest plan to hold it for her. Bangs's judgment is very good in these matters, and I infer from the way he writes that he thinks we would probably decide to keep it."

"I am inclined to think as you do," said Mr. Dexter; "it is evident that Mr. Bangs thinks the property will appreciate in value."

"Well, then, I will wire Bangs to wait for letter,

and will write him to place the villa in proper
hands for rent, and to convert the other securities
into cash according to his best judgment."

Thus unknown to Nettie, she became the sole
owner of a beautiful Roman villa.

·

CHAPTER XII.

Mrs. Tillottson remembers an Old Friend—Mr. Campion provided for—The Van Twists visit Cup Island—Plans for an
Open-air Tea-party—Jack to deliver an Address.

"Why, Mr. Campion is coming to Oldport," said
Nettie to the others, as they sat in the summer-
house one pleasant afternoon; "and he is coming
on Thursday," she continued, then again looking
at a letter from her uncle which she had just received, she read aloud as follows:

"I think, Nettie, that Camp"—"Uncle always
calls him Camp," she explained—"has missed you
almost as much as I, at any rate he says he is
going to Oldport for a few days for his health.
He will give you the latest news from home, and
be with you on Thursday next. Take good care
of the dear old elephant, and see that he is not
attacked with home-sickness."

"Who is Mr. Campion?" asked Tom, a curious feeling shooting keenly through him.

"Mr. Campion is uncle's dearest friend," said Nettie.

"Is his name Augustus Campion?" Mrs. Tillottson asked.

"Why, yes; but how did you know?" said Nettie, smiling.

"He was a classmate of your father's, my dear," said Mrs. Tillottson, addressing her daughter, then turning to Nettie she said, pleasantly, "I shall always remember Augustus Campion with respect and admiration. My husband was very fond of him. I think he was the most unselfish or rather the most thoughtful man for others that I ever met. I am very glad that we shall so soon have the pleasure of seeing him; but how is his wife?"

"Mrs. Campion died at least five years ago," said Nettie; "and he has but one child, a daughter about my own age, and one of my very dear friends. Belle knows her. I wish he would bring Josephine with him, but uncle writes that she is now at Long Branch with her uncle's family. I suppose she will spend the summer there at their cottage."

"Yes," said Mrs. Tillottson; "that is Charles Campion, who married Josephine Brooks, one of my New York friends. Mr. Campion has been quite a successful lawyer, has he not?"

"Oh, yes, indeed," said Nettie; "uncle says he has the best practice in our part of the State, and that he is one of our wealthiest citizens; but no one would ever suspect it, for he is a very modest man, and attends closely to his legal business. By the way, Uncle Adam advises me to look for a place where Mr. Campion can have a room."

"Yes," said Mrs. Tillottson, "that is advisable; but, of course, he must eat his meals with us, if possible. Thomas, I think you had better go over at once and ask Mrs. Sandy if she will accommodate him. I think that she will probably let him have the room that we vacated, which is very comfortable."

"All right," said the doctor, rising, and glad enough to be of service to Nettie; "I will go at once, as Sandy will also be pretty sure to be at home at this time."

"And I will go with you," said Nettie, springing to her feet and wrapping her shawl about her; "for I feel very anxious to be certain about accommodations for Uncle Camp, and, besides, I desire to write an answer to my letter about it this evening if possible."

"Don't be away long," said Mrs. Tillottson; "for Bid will ring the tea-bell in a few moments."

"Tell her to blow the horn," said Tom; "and if we hear it we will hurry back."

"Very well," said his mother, smiling.

"How old is your friend, Mr. Campion?" asked Tom of Nettie, as he was pulling the boat across the water.

"Give a guess," said Nettie, mischievously.

"Well, I will guess ninety-seven years."

"Too old by far," she replied. "Did you think that because I call him uncle, and because he is a widower, he must be a Methuselah?"

"Sixty," said Tom.

"Too old again," said Nettie, decisively. "Why, he is as active and energetic as you are."

"Thirty-five," said Tom, in despair.

"Wrong again;" and Nettie could no longer restrain her mirth. "Mr. Campion,—or Uncle Camp, as I have always called him ever since I was a child and sat upon his knee and listened to the delightful stories he used to tell,—Uncle Camp is just uncle's age, and Uncle Adam was fifty-seven last May."

Tom felt relieved, and showed his improved condition by an attempt to change the subject.

"Well, we must contrive to get pleasant rooms for him if possible," he said, cheerfully. "Do you know I have a strong liking already for your Uncle Camp? Is he a little man?"

This question brought another hearty laugh from Nettie.

"Oh, Dr. Tillottson," she said, pathetically, "you will be careful with him, won't you, he is so

very tiny and delicate. Why, when I stand up so"
—here she stood up in the boat, at the imminent
risk of capsizing them both—"and hold out my
arm so"—more risk and a "look out" from Tom—
"he can easily walk right under it without touching a hair of his head."

Mr. Campion was several inches over six feet in
height, and in weight was probably as heavy as
Tom and Nettie combined. Of course, Nettie
meant that he could pass under her arm by
stooping; besides, Mr. Campion's head on the
top was as smooth and free from hair as a new
billiard-ball.

"I like little men," said Tom, roguishly; "there
is something so pathetic, so appealing, about them;
you always feel as though being bankrupt in avoir-
dupois, they should be indulged and treated with
kindness."

"Well, I hope you will be kind to dear little
Uncle Camp," said Nettie; "although I must say
there is nothing very pathetic about him."

Mr. and Mrs. Sandy were both at home, and
freely expressed their perfect willingness to accommodate another boarder.

"Bless my soul, I remember Mr. Campion well,"
said Sandy, who seemed delighted; "an' a jolly
Dick he was, too. He kem here twelve years ago
next November, with yer daddy, Dorkter; an' a
cleaner shot never drawed a bead on a duck. I'll

be mighty glad ter see him." So Nettie and Tom left the Sandy cottage with the pleasing conviction that Mr. Campion would receive a hearty welcome there at any rate.

"I suppose I saw your Uncle Camp when he was here before, if Sandy is right," said Tom; "but I cannot recall his appearance. If I remember right, all of my father's friends on those ducking parties were large men; but, of course, a boy will not form correct ideas of size."

Nettie smiled. "If it is easy to remember large men," said she, "it is probably difficult to recollect small ones; but you will not easily forget Uncle Camp again when you see him, he is so very jolly."

It was evident that Nettie liked to tease.

One afternoon, not long after this, Mrs. Van Twist and her daughter were rowed over to Cup Island, to return the visit which Belle and Nettie had made them.

The ladies all received them cordially, the gentlemen being absent on some sailing-trip. After highly praising the coziness of their cottage Mrs. Van Twist, in the course of her conversation, said,—

"My cousin, Mr. Van Dusen, has been very kind to us all."

"Yes, indeed," said Mrs. Tillottson; "we feel very grateful to him for his hospitality, and for the many little courtesies which he has extended to us. I sincerely wish it was in our power to return some of his kindness."

"How would it do for us to give a lawn-party?" said Belle. "It seems to me it would be delightful on some moonlight evening."

"Unfortunately, we have no lawn," said her mother, "and it would be impossible to entertain many in our small cottage."

"I have it," said Alice Van Twist, with emphasis. "We will give an open-air tea-party upon Smoke Island, sending each gentleman a written invitation, worded something like this: 'The ladies of Cup and Smoke Islands request the pleasure of your presence at an open-air tea-party upon Smoke Island on Saturday next, if pleasant, at five P.M.'"

"That is a very good idea," said Mrs. Van Twist. "I think we will be able to give them enjoyment."

The others assented to this plan, each one agreeing to do something toward making it a success. The refreshments were to be furnished by the ladies of both islands. Belle volunteered to decorate some cake; Nettie was to look after the tea; Miss Van Twist said she would have some lobster salad, and invited the girls to come over early on Saturday to assist in decorating their cottage. It was also planned that after the tea there should be a musical performance upon the water, which was to consist of a vocal quartette by Tom, Jack, Belle, and Nettie; a solo by Miss Van Twist to banjo accompaniment, and a duet to banjo accompaniment by Belle and Jack, after which they were all to visit Cup Island, where Mr. Stratton would deliver an address.

"Oh, he will do it," said Belle, in reply to a question from her mother as to whether Jack would consent; "he can do anything that he sets his mind to."

"I have no doubt but that it will be done well if he does it at all," said Mrs. Tillottson. "We will also ask Mr. Campion to make us a speech; he is a splendid speaker, and one of the most humorous and original men that I ever met."

"Oh, yes," said Nettie; "that will be splendid; Uncle Camp is so very funny when he is having a good time."

These and some other plans were made and agreed to by all of the ladies, after which the Van Twists left, much pleased at the result of their visit, and resolved to do all in their power to make the tea-party a success.

CHAPTER XIII.

The Sail to Millville Light—Blue-fishing—Captain and Mrs. l'arkins entertain—Jack talks with a Parrot—Jack opens his Heart—Belle's Tongue is loosened—Mr. Campion arrives— He makes a Confidante of Mrs. Tillottson.

IT happened that Mr. Van Dusen had invited the Cup Island party and the Van Twists to visit Captain Parkins at the Millville light-house, on the very day when Mr. Campion was to arrive at Oldport. On this account Nettie hesitated some about going, but was finally persuaded, after instructing Sandy to meet him at the station with the wagon. Mrs. Tillottson concluded to stay at home, which also somewhat eased Nettie's mind.

The sail on the "Siren" was delightful. They left Oldport Harbor about eight o'clock, on one of those mornings which, in the heat of summer, are so charming upon the water. The air was cool and full of invigorating freshness. On their way they threw over several blue-fish lines, trolling for blue-fish. The fish that morning seemed particularly voracious, for hardly had the first line, which was Belle's, been out a moment, before a six-pound fish was pulling vigorously at the other end. Belle shouted for assistance, for the strain upon the stout line was too much for her delicate feminine hands. Jack and Mr. Craik, who were usually at hand whenever she needed anything, both responded, and the fish was soon landed struggling and gasping upon the clean white deck of the yacht, where it was turned over to the charge of a sailor. Nettie's line had by this time been thrown out, and in a moment or two all were eagerly holding their lines in the exciting expectation of a struggle with fish.

Trolling is by no means tame sport, when the fish are punctual to bite and of lusty size; and as the boat sails swiftly through the water under a stiff breeze, there is plenty of excitement in having a struggling, vigorous six- or eight-pounder pulling at the far end of sixty or eighty feet of line; now rushing toward the boat with surprising speed, the fish will slacken the line for a moment, giving one the impression that it has parted and the fish has escaped, till suddenly, with a quick jerk, he is felt travelling in another direction, and the taut line threatens to cut through the heavy leather or canvas mittens, which it is always policy to wear upon these occasions. But, when, after slowly and surely pulling him in " hand over hand" until he can be seen, a long flash of pale blue light darting, now to one side, now to the other, and then, perhaps, jumping in frantic efforts several feet out of the water, until finally with a steady quick pull he is landed safely on deck, one feels that the effort is well repaid.

When Belle had landed the first fish, Mr. Van Dusen had the yacht put about, and they sailed through the school several times, consuming considerable time, but catching altogether fifteen good-sized beauties.

Later they dined upon the yacht, and had the pleasure of eating some of the fish which they had caught. During the excitement, and after Belle's good fortune, Tom found opportunity to ask Nettie if she did not think she could hasten her luck by again transforming him into a fish.

" No," said Nettie; " for you would be sure to be too loquacious, and, of course, could not bite and talk at the same time; besides, I mean soon to catch a large fish." The words were scarcely uttered before, sure enough, she was surprised by a rude jerk at the line, pulling her arms out straight, and reminding her that it requires strength to hold a good-sized, angry blue-fish. Tom laughingly helped her pull in the line, advising her now and then how to handle it, until the fish was close under the stern of the yacht, when she, knowing herself incapable of landing such a monster, relinquished it, and he, with a strong lift, brought safely to the deck a noble specimen weighing in the scales just eight pounds and five ounces, and the largest capture, so it proved, of the day.

When the yacht arrived off the Millville light-house, Mr. Van Dusen ordered the sailors to load and fire the little brass cannon, which brought into sight Captain Parkins, who waved his hat from the beach in acknowledgment of the salute.

They then went ashore in the yawl, and were all introduced by Jack and Tom to the captain and his good wife. Mrs. Parkins invited them into the house, which was a neat little cottage, built at the rear of and adjoining the light-house proper. This latter was a round monumental structure of great height, built of brick, and painted white.

After enjoying and praising the excellence of some cider and "doughnuts," which were furnished by Mrs. Parkins, they were escorted up into the tall, white tower adjoining, where the captain uncovered the immense crystals which refract and radiate the powerful light, explaining to them the accurate adjustment of clock-work by which the beacon is shut off or exposed at regular intervals, and giving them varied information in regard to the light-house service.

They did not stay up in the tower long, however, for the intense heat of the sun made doubly powerful by the reflection of the heavy plate-glass windows, which surround the circular apartment, and the strong odor of oil, did not help to rivet attention to the captain's words, particularly that of the young ladies; so after enduring it as long as they could, they cut short the captain's enthusiastic eulogium upon lights and light-houses in general by leading the way to terra-firma.

Separating into groups they strolled about the neighborhood, if such it could be called, for it was simply a cape or point, with a long, sloping sandy beach, and here or there a cluster of immense black rocks, against which the waves were beating with a persistent roar. The Van Twists, Mr. Van Dusen, and Craik followed Mrs. Parkins. Mr. Kendall and the professor went with the captain to the east side of the point, where he promised to show them the remains of a large schooner which had been driven upon the rocks early in the season. Tom and Nettie were, as usual, after shells and mosses along the shore; Aunt Deb had squatted herself upon the beach under an umbrella, declaring that she would not budge another step, while Jack and Belle sat in the shadow of the cottage and amused themselves by talking and listening to a beautiful parrot, which the captain had brought from the Indies a number of years previous. Jack opened quite a sociable conversation with the bird, who, however, insisted upon talking in Spanish the greater part of the time. Here is a sample of their conversation:

Jack: " Hello, Polly."

Polly: " Ha, ha, ha," followed by a prolonged whistle.

Jack: "Ha, ha, ha," and a prolonged whistle.

Polly: "Ha. Que hora es? Pretty bird."

Jack: "Yes, pretty bird. What did you say, Polly?"

Polly, trying to bite Jack's finger: "Mal tempo muy malo muchacho."

Jack: "Ha, ha! Why Poll, that isn't English."

Polly: "Get out! Hurry up! Oh-h-h-h! Oh-h-h-h-h!" A whistle. "Que quiere usted?" and so on, Polly always getting the upper hand in the argument, for Jack's Spanish was none of the best.

Then leaving the bird they strolled down upon the sandy beach, where they sat in the shadow of a huge rock listening to the roar of the waters, and watching the graceful sea-gulls sailing about them in the air. They were both very happy. Belle knew that Jack adored her, for since their first meeting he had told her so by a thousand little spontaneous demonstrations, which were as plain to her as so many words. Thus they sat loving and silent, when suddenly Jack's manner changed. He became very communicative and nervous in his actions one moment, and the next would be absent-minded, and apparently ill at ease. Belle, with accurate feminine wisdom, knew that he was having an inward struggle with himself, and would soon tell her of his love. She pitied him, and something in the expression of her beautiful face encouraged him to stammer out,—

"Miss Tillottson, Isabel, you must know by this time that I love you, that I worship the very ground beneath your feet."

Jack hesitated a moment from sheer excitement, and Belle felt her hot brows throbbing with every heart-beat.

"I have thought," he continued, "sometimes that perhaps it would be unfair for me to speak of this during our stay at Cup Island, but since the arrival of your dear mother I have been encouraged to tell you my secret. In fact, I can no longer hold it; I must speak." Then seeing that Belle's face bore an expression of great joy, he said, taking her hand between both of his own, "Belle, my darling, tell me that my love is returned."

Belle's hand remained where it was, but she could not speak; the blood, which at first had left her cheeks ashy pale, now came crowding in rich color into her beautiful face; her whole soul was overcome with emotion, and two great tears of joy stealing out from the downcast lids, dropped upon Jack's hand.

"Quick, my darling," he said, "tell me that you love me."

Belle's head, which had been bending lower and lower, gave a little involuntary nod of assent, and the next moment it was lying upon his breast, while he clasped her lovingly to him.

The waves kept on their sorrowful song, and the gulls continued to circle about them in the air, but these two lovers knew it not. A new world had thrown wide its portals to them. Life was just beginning.

Belle's tongue was now loosened, indeed it was remarkably glib. She told Jack how dearly she had loved him from the first, and he kissed her for that; she told him how she feared and had tried to avoid Craik, and he kissed her for that; probably, if she had told him that his moustache was on fire, he would have sealed the information in the same ardent manner.

He told her, in return, of his hopes and fears; how he had passed many of the long nights in wakefulness, sometimes sitting in the cool starlight under her window, sometimes lying in his bunk at the cottage, but always with his thoughts fixed upon her, his angel; and then he kissed her for being his angel.

It was agreed between them that until he had spoken with her mother, and for the present, their engagement was to be kept a secret. They were very happy as they returned to the cottage where the others were awaiting them, and a pang shot through the breast of Craik as he saw them approaching side by side, for he could not help realizing in a measure how matters stood with them. He was very attentive, however, to Belle during the return sail, striving in every manner to win her regard. It was well for Belle that she was strong, for Craik had a most winning way with women, which, aided by his remarkably handsome face and figure, had scored for him many a victory. But we know Belle too well to even for a moment think that she could waver from the noble instincts of her nature.

She was truly a woman, not a coquette. Like most women, she had an eye for beauty and a taste for refinement, and at first she had greatly admired those qualities in Craik ; but in the accurate scales of her feminine judgment they never weighed a feather's weight against Jack, with his honest outspoken ways and joyous disposition. She seemed to read the inner man in Craik as she was thrown more and more in his society, aided by little remarks which he would make from time to time when temporarily off his guard.

The following is a sample of the manner in which he would expose himself to her inspection. As they sailed homeward the sea, which was a trifle rough, occasionally broke across the bow of the yacht, throwing a spray over the whole deck. The first time that this happened Jack, who had found a shawl belonging to Belle, threw it with a knowing smile into her lap, and she placed it about her thinly-clad shoulders to protect her from future showers. Craik, who sat close beside her, made a motion to assist her in adjusting the shawl, but she declined his assistance, saying, as she did so, that she was accustomed to waiting upon herself.

"But you would not object, I suppose, to having a handy dressing-maid?" said Craik.

"Yes, I should most decidedly," said Belle. "Of course, if I was unable to arrange my own toilet the case might be different, but while I have health and strength I prefer to wait upon myself. Still, I do not object to the employment of a maid by others; tastes differ greatly, and it would be wrong to lay down a rule for all."

"I thought all women delighted in being waited upon," said Craik.

"Not all," said Belle; "some delight in waiting upon others."

"Oh, yes, when they are married, of course," said Craik, laughing.

Belle understood the drift of his remark, but she could not laugh. She had spoken honestly, unselfishly, and had meant that many good women love to be of use to their fellow-creatures; but the beauty of this thought had been entirely lost upon Craik, whose idea of feminine usefulness was confined to that of a wife to her husband. It was in this way and many others that Craik had betrayed the selfishness of his nature, and Belle could see

22

the cruelty that lurked beneath a pleasing exterior.

Jack was in ecstasy, and it did Belle's heart good to see how happy she had made him. He told funny stories to Mrs. Van Twist, smoked a cigar with Van Dusen, made the major laugh until he had the hiccoughs, started up lively songs in which they all joined, and helped the sailors in the management of the yacht, all the time keeping a wary eye of affectionate regard upon Belle. It seemed impossible for him to sit still a moment. Belle, who was talking with Craik, would occasionally find her attention attracted by a general laugh, and on investigating the cause would invariably find that it was Jack. He sprawled himself out upon the narrow bowsprit at the imminent risk of a ducking in the sound, singing meantime at the top of his voice snatches from the popular operas of the day. He climbed the rigging until the ladies, with fear depicted upon their faces, implored him to come down ; he walked the deck pretending to be " half seas over," begging charity from the others, and stating in the spluttering language of a drunken wretch that he was an honest sailor walking from San Francisco to Boston to see his wife and children, who " God bless them are dyin' to see their daddy."

He imitated every variety of animal known to Barnum, and some that neither Barnum nor any

mortal ever saw or heard. He borrowed Aunt
Deb's "specs" and, mounting a stool, preached a
sermon upon the "frailty of human expectations,"
which greatly amused Belle, and somewhat dis-
concerted Craik. It was evident to all that Jack
was happy. There were but two people on board,
however, who really suspected the cause; and
these were Tom and Nettie. Miss Van Twist was
enjoying the excursion also, for Mr. Kendall had
been very attentive to her during the day.

Mr. Kendall had surprised himself by discovering many hidden virtues in Miss Van Twist; and,
strange as it may seem, this young woman possessed
in a corner of her nature an innate taste for Sunday-
school, church, and missionary work; it seemed
to develop in her, under his encouragement, like a
weed in the sun. It was remarkable; and her fond
mother gazed with a feeling of maternal pride and
admiration, well mixed with amazement, as she
heard her draw the reverend young gentleman
out upon these important topics. It was phe-
nomenal. Mr. Kendall considered himself a man
of unusual penetration, and it proved that he was
right, especially when the object of his favor was
so clever a lady as Alice Van Twist, and withal so
extremely pleasing to his masculine vanity.

So they thoroughly enjoyed the day together,
these two young people; and when Miss Van Twist
tried to sleep that night she found that her eyes

would pop open, and that, open or shut, they always brought her visions of Mr. Kendall's handsome beard, and Mr. Kendall's fine eyes.

Meantime Mr. Campion arrived in Oldport; was met by Mr. Sandy, and conveyed with his baggage to Sandy's house. After taking dinner and smoking his customary cigar, he went with Sandy to Cup Island, where he was welcomed by Mrs. Tillottson, who was expecting him. As we have before intimated, Mrs. Tillottson was one of his ardent admirers. He had been a true friend of her husband's, and in the early days of her married life they had seen much of each other.

It was now over fifteen years since they had met, and each had some curiosity to know how time had treated the other.

"Well, well, Mary," said Mr. Campion, "is it indeed you? Why, you look as though your life had been spent among rose-leaves and infant angels."

"Among roses and infants, perhaps," said Mrs. Tillottson, laughing, as they seated themselves under the shade of the chestnut-trees, in front of the little cottage; "but I am looking better than I was a few weeks ago at home. I was actually driven from home by my physician, who insisted that I needed salt air; and it proves he was right, for I feel so remarkably well here, and we are having such pleasant times, that I am inclined to

stay forever. Has your health been good all of
these long years? But I need not ask; I can see
for myself that you are as well and strong as ever.
How is your daughter, Josephine?"

"Well, quite well," he replied, "when last I
heard from her a few days ago. This is the same
old fascinating spot, Mary, and it seems but yesterday since we were here, your dear husband, Tom,
bless his memory, the life of the party, and all in-
tent upon the capture of fish and the slaughter
of ducks."

Thus they continued to talk of old times until
the conversation gradually drifted upon the events
of the present; then he told her about the death
of Roger Dexter, about Mr. Dexter's serious illness, and the object of his visit to Oldport, about
his suspicions of Craik, in fact everything; for as
he proceeded he felt that same inclination to make
a confidante of her, which people generally felt who
once thoroughly knew her. She listened patiently,
the tears coming and going in her beautiful eyes,
as he touched upon the pathetic portions of his
story, and, finally, when he had informed her of
Mr. Dexter's desire to keep Nettie in ignorance
for awhile of these events, especially that of his
illness, she said, feelingly,—

"I think your friend is a noble man. Nettie has
a large and tender heart, and it will save her much
pain to keep these unfortunate facts from her for a

time, especially as her uncle is improving so
rapidly. As to this man Craik, I have struggled
against an overwhelming antipathy against him
ever since he came. I am sure he is the man you
seek, for I have frequently noticed the very deformity of the little finger which you have mentioned. But what will you do now? Arrest
him?"

"No, I think not," said Mr. Campion, "at least
not immediately; he is connected with a regular
organized band of thieves, some of whom are
working in this country at present. The authorities with whom I am in correspondence are anxious
to unearth as many of these rascals as possible,
and have already woven the net which will capture
them, but a little time is necessary, and meantime
I have made up my mind to stay here as a sort of
protection to you and the girls, and at the same
time to watch this crafty outlaw. Of course,
Mary, you understand—in fact, it is unnecessary
for me to tell you—that these facts which I have
mentioned are secrets, and to be kept in strict
confidence from every one for the present."

CHAPTER XIV.

Craik Outwitted—Tom and Nettie become Cupid's Unconscious
Victims—A Touching Scene in the Summer-house—The Tea-
party—Jack's Address, and Aunt Deb's Suggestions—A Silent
Declaration.

MR. CAMPION spent the greater part of his time
after this upon Cup Island. He would breakfast
at the Sandy cottage, then leisurely read his mail,
smoke a cigar, and peruse the daily papers, when,
it being by this time about nine or ten o'clock, he
would take a boat and row himself over to the
Tillottson cottage.

The addition of Augustus Campion to their
family circle was a happy circumstance for them
all: he was as full of animal spirits as Jack:
genial, fond of anecdote, as generous of impulse
as a child, he gave himself up wholly to the enjoyment of this invigorating life by the sea.

He was presented to Van Dusen and his guests
shortly after his arrival, and by his gentlemanly
bearing, genial disposition, and sensible remarks
soon won their respect and admiration. Van
Dusen already knew him by reputation, and was
proud to invite him to the yacht as often as
possible. Fishing parties were planned and car-

ried out, in which he participated, and he was the
central figure of most of the merry-makings; but
it might have been noticed, had any one been so
disposed, that he always went wherever Craik did.
If Craik stayed at home, upon the "Siren," Mr.
Campion was not far away upon Cup Island. On
no occasion, when he could possibly avoid it, did
Mr. Campion allow Craik to interview any of the
Cup Island ladies alone, and he was constantly
aided in this good work by Mrs. Tillottson, who
used all of her woman's tact to assist him in
carrying out his plans.

She was often of great service to him in thus
closely watching Craik's movements. If he came
to Cup Island, and Mr. Campion was at Oldport,
she had a signal by which she could notify him of
the fact, when he would immediately take his boat
and row over. If, when the men were going on a
fishing excursion, Craik, at the last moment, decided to stay at home, Mrs. Tillottson would plan
some excuse for Mr. Campion to remain also.
Thus matters went along for a week or so. The
lawyer had taken the first opportunity which
offered to compare Craik with the picture he carried in his pocket; he had also noticed the deformity of the little finger, and was now thoroughly
convinced that he was no other than Bolan, or
Gentleman Jim. As soon as he was satisfied about
this, he had written to Ferris telling him all of the

particulars, and advising him not to hurry Craik's arrest, but to capture, if possible, all of the gang he could discover, and informing him that it was Van Dusen's intention to stay in the vicinity of Oldport for several weeks. It was a great relief to Belle that Mr. Campion kept in the constant society of Craik, for Jack was often away upon some excursion with the gentlemen, and Craik tried to make these occasions opportunities for him to press his attentions upon her. Mr. Campion saw all of this planning on Craik's part, and, aided by Mrs. Tillottson, always succeeded in foiling his intentions. Craik was puzzled and much put out. At first he had been inclined to fancy the lawyer, whose easy manners, jolly stories and jokes went far to relieve what seemed to him a slow, monotonous life; but as he found his efforts to throw himself into the good graces of Miss Tillottson all cleverly thwarted, and always by this good-natured man, he began to suspect him, and dislike was soon added to suspicion in his estimate of the lawyer. Why should he always be in the way? He was too old to be considered much of a rival, but he was nevertheless an intolerable nuisance. If he could only get this Campion interested in the Van Twists, he would then have a better chance with the girls. He would try. Perhaps Mrs. Van Twist would bite at the bait if he could but think of some way to get her to do it. Campion was a

very wealthy man. He would tell Mrs. Van Twist
this, and hint that he had noticed that Campion
greatly admired her daughter Alice. That might
do it. Campion was a widower, and the Van Twists
would probably jump at the chance of having a
man of his wealth and reputation for a son-in-law.
They would invite him over to Smoke Island and
treat him so nicely that he would probably spend a
good part of his time there; this would leave him
a chance to see more of Miss Tillottson alone.

But this plot of Craik's was not a success. Mrs.
Van Twist was very cordial with the lawyer, and
did, indeed, press him to come to Smoke Island
often, even going so far as to plot for the accomplishment of her designs; but Mr. Campion did
not in the least relax his vigilance over the two
girls: wherever they went, if Craik was on hand,
he went also, unless Jack and Tom accompanied
them.

Jack had taken the first opportunity to inform
Mrs. Tillottson of his love for her daughter, and
she had willingly given her consent, for she was
not taken by surprise; her mother's watchful eye
had long since noticed Jack's partiality for her
daughter, and, besides, she had formed a strong
friendship for Jack. He was her boy's best friend.
Indeed, to her it seemed a fortunate event that one
so well beloved by them all as Jack should offer
himself. Besides, she had a dread of Mr. Craik;

not that she was afraid that Belle was in danger
of being influenced by Craik, still he was so persistent in his attentions that she feared him. She
also felt that, as the affianced wife of Mr. Stratton,
her daughter was safer from such a villain; for,
thanks to Mr. Campion, such she now knew Craik
to be.

Tom was let into the secret of the engagement,
Belle confided it to Nettie, and naturally Mrs.
Tillottson informed Mr. Campion, for she felt that
it might be unfair or unwise to keep him in ignorance, particularly when he had taken her so fully
into his confidence. Between Tom and Nettie,
therefore, the subject of the engagement became a
matter of frequent discussion. Tom was delighted
that his sister had fallen into such good hands,
and was profuse in his praises to Nettie. Nettie,
too, was pleased that Belle had found so much
happiness, and her pleasure increased as she
learned from Tom Jack's true character. Naturally these confidences brought them into a closer
and more friendly intimacy. It became a matter
of custom or habit with Tom to consult Nettie
about the little questions which were constantly
cropping up in their rustic life. If there was a
doubt about the wisdom of doing this thing or
that, on their daily expeditions by boat or land,
Tom and Nettie were sure to have their heads
close together in friendly exchange of opinions.

It was readily seen what this was leading to, and our wise reader has, no doubt, already inferred that Tom and Nettie were to make a match; and so it was in fact; but they were doing it as thousands of the most felicitous matches are made nowadays in America. Unconsciously and in an innocent spirit, as free from guile as the wooing of a pair of turtle-doves, they were deeply in love. The genuineness of their love made their courtship instinctive. There were no formal passes of etiquette between these two natures. We might almost truly say that they became affianced by slips of the tongue, prompted by the natural action of their loving hearts. Neither was there any secrecy in their wooing; it was as evident to outsiders as is the love-song of a canary. Of course, there were a thousand little love-passages between them which were unnoticed by the outside world, but there was no effort to conceal even these, in fact the lovers were in a measure unconscious that they were happening. Tom's first question on his return from a fishing-trip was, "Where is Nettie?" and Nettie's first look in the morning, and last at night, were for Tom. They had long since addressed each other as Tom and Nettie, and it seemed to be understood by all except, perhaps, themselves, that they were lovers.

The preparations for the party upon Smoke Island had all been made, and at the appointed

time the guests were assembled at three hand-
somely-decorated tables, which were placed in the
shade of the Van Twist cottage. It was about six
o'clock when they sat down to enjoy the dainties
which the ingenuity and skill of the ladies had
prepared. Mr. Campion was as usual in high
spirits, as was also Jack. Mr. Van Dusen was
delighted, and all seemed to really enjoy the fes-
tivity save Craik, who, deprived of a seat by Belle,
made no effort to entertain his next neighbor, who
happened to be Mrs. Van Twist. Mr. Kendall,
aware that the bright eyes of Alice Van Twist
were upon him, outshone himself in gallantry and
good-nature, while the professor chatted with Mrs.
Tillottson in a most social manner, each moment
discovering in her new beauties of mind and soul.
Bid was brought into requisition to assist the Van
Twist domestics in waiting upon the tables, and
the ladies were well satisfied to see everything
run so smoothly.

Of course, Tom and Nettie sat together, he indulging in the usual jokes with which lovers
delight to entertain the objects of their devotion.

Jack, as usual, was brimming over with fun; he
made temporary visits to the different tables, con-
vulsing the guests with laughter wherever he went.

They lingered for two hours over the repast;
the gentlemen finally lighting their cigars, after
which they all adjourned to the shore to hear the

vocal quartette, which was creditably performed by our four young people from Cup Island. They embarked in one of the small boats, and, rowing out on the still waters, now just beginning to be lighted up by the new moon, sang "Sweet and Low" so admirably that they received a hearty *encore* from the audience upon the beach. Jack then sang a merry air to a banjo accompaniment; Miss Van Twist displayed some taste and a fair voice by singing a very sweet solo, after which the whole party went over to Cup Island to hear the addresses.

Jack was fully equal to the occasion. He mounted a chair, and amused the guests for at least a half-hour. Occasional interruptions by Aunt Deborah added zest to the amusement, and were enjoyed by Jack as much as the others.

He began his speech by assuming the rôle of a stump-speaker on politics.

"Why is it," said he, after the usual introductory remarks, "that our glorious country can hold her head higher than the proudest nations of the world? Why is it every native-born American citizen can sit around his hearthstone or can milk his cow in peaceful confidence fearing no interruption?"

"No more can he allus," said Aunt Deborah; "fur some cows kick like fury, an' a pail o' milk is no heavier to them than a—than a——"

"Than a foot-ball to a Yale student," interrupted Jack. "I referred though, more particularly, to foreign interruptions." Jack was delighted that Aunt Deborah showed a disposition to be merry, as it gave him time to think.

"Now here are the women of the country," he continued, changing his tactics, "trying to smuggle themselves into politics, and to control the destiny of this glorious republic. Why is it?"—here he looked hard at Aunt Deb.—"Why are they so anxious to deprive the weaker masculine element of its acquired rights?"

"Whew! guess you're a little mixed about that, Mr. Speaker," said Aunt Deb; "fur in all my life-long experience I never saw a woman try to vote. Why, they'd be skeered to death at meetin' a lot o' men folks at the polls."

"It is conceded," continued Jack, very seriously, "that the proper sphere for woman is the mission-ary field; they are our natural teachers, and it is a matter of profound congratulation that so many noble-hearted maidens are enlisting in this com-mendable service."

"Well, well," said Aunt Deb; "'xcuse me, but I must put in a word right here. Missionary service may be a very good thing for them as can't get a bite o' bread or a roof to cover their heads in their own country; but, deary me, to think of a respectably raised female leavin' her

own kith an' kin an' rushin' off to Afriky or
Chiny, is 'nough to make one ashamed of her own
sex.   Why, there was Mandy Jinks of our town;
she took the missionary fever bad a few years ago,
when one o' them slick an' slippery talkers was
there, an' the very next year she toted off to the
East Indies.   We ladies of the church helped fit
her out nice, I tell you, leastwise what we could
do by sewin', an' she went off as proud as a young
kitten with a dead mouse; but bless ye, she hadn't
ben gone over a year when we began to get the
pitifulest letters from her beggin' to come home,
an', the next thing, home she came, an' a shabby-
lookin' mortal she was.   Deliver me from missionary service; but I'm afeered I'm a-interruptin'
of ye, Mr. Stratton."

Jack continued his speech, causing much amusement, and, after he had finished, Mr. Campion was
asked to make a short address.   This he did very
gracefully and cordially.   He thanked the ladies
for the delightful manner in which they had made
time pleasant for them all, and as Aunt Deborah
expressed it afterwards, " He was jest the slickest
speechifier" she ever heard.

One morning, some weeks after this occurrence,
Nettie was pressing mosses out in the summer-
house upon Bogus Island, where Tom had rigged
up for her a crude but effective press, consisting
of two heavy pine boards and a large flat stone,

which he always adjusted upon them for her when she had any mosses to press.

This time, however, she was alone; she had placed her mosses between the leaves of an old book, and not seeing Tom, who had not returned from a trip to Oldport, she attempted to lift the stone upon the boards herself; it was while she was in the act of doing this that Tom entered the summer-house and hastened to her assistance; but before he had reached her the rock in some manner slipped, falling heavily against her foot. She gave a little cry of distress, and hearing his approach attempted to rise to her feet, but the agony which she experienced from the bruised foot was too much for her, and she would have fallen to the floor had not Tom sprang forward and caught her in his arms. The injury to her foot was not at all serious, and the pain was but momentary, so that she was quickly herself again, and in a laughing tone said, "What a goose I was, Tom, to attempt to lift that heavy stone. There, thank you, I am all right now," then glancing up into his face, for his strong arms were still about her, she saw tears of true sympathy glittering in his eyes. Tom could not reply; his heart was overflowing with affection for her, and the expression of love and sympathy which she saw in his handsome eyes could not be mistaken. She hid her face in his breast. Not a word was spoken. There they

stood, these nature's children, heart throbbing
against heart, affianced by a hand mightier than
man's; and when at last Tom said, gently stroking
her soft black hair, " Nettie, my darling," she drew
even closer to him and whispered, " Don't talk,
Tom, dear."

Let us no longer intrude upon the sacredness
of such a scene. Words are powerless to describe
the beauties of such innocent affection; they
convey but a faint idea, and generally an imperfect
and misleading one.

An author whom we all have learned to love
has said,—

" I have made a book or two in my time, and I
am making another that perhaps will see the light
one of these days. But, if I had my life to live
over again, I think I should go in for silence, and
get as near to *Nirvana* as I could. This language
is such a paltry tool. The handle of it cuts, and
the blade doesn't. You muddle yourself by not
knowing what you mean by a word, and send out
your unanswered riddles and rebuses to clear up
other people's difficulties. It always seems to me
that talk is a ripple, and thought a ground swell.
A string of words that mean pretty much . anything helps you in a certain sense to get hold of
a thought, just as a string of syllables that mean
nothing helps you to a word; but it is a poor
business, it's a poor business, and the more you

study *definition* the more you find out how poor
it is."

So instead of dwelling upon the ecstatic bliss
radiating between those two loving souls, we will
leave them to the tender mercies of our gentle
readers, knowing that a clearer conception of their
heavenly condition will be reached by them in
dreaming over the resources and experiences of
their own diverse natures; in some, sweet visions
of the past, in others, delights of the present, and
in still others, ideal capacities which anticipate
future fulfilments.

CHAPTER XV.

Night on Oldport Harbor—A Desperate Struggle and a Capture
—Mr. Campion utilizes his Muscle—Mr. Van Dusen Indig-
nant—An Explanation—Ferris Happy—Cup Island becomes
deserted.

It was night. All was darkness upon Oldport
Harbor. Even the stars were hidden behind a
veil of sombre-looking clouds; and as the eye
tried to penetrate the distance in the direction of
Cup Island, it was met by a black wall of pitchy
gloom, through which nothing could be seen.
One solitary light was visible upon the Harbor;
this sent its feeble ray from the little lantern

which hung upon the "Siren." It was two
o'clock in the morning. Sandy's cottage looked
dark and uninviting, the outside blinds were
tightly closed for the night. But all was not
darkness inside. Let us look in. There are five
men sitting in the little front room. We recognize Mr. Sandy, the tall dignified form of Mr.
Campion, and Ferris, the Chicago detective. The
other two are unknown to us. They are employed
by Ferris. After a short consultation, four of
these five men leave the Sandy cottage, and, led by
Mr. Campion, make their way through the darkness to the wharf, where they silently embark in a
row-boat, and as quietly pull in the direction of
the little beacon which seems to beckon them to
the "Siren." Van Dusen and his guests are all
sound asleep upon the yacht, the watch upon
deck only being partly conscious of time and
worldly affairs, as the little boat draws gently
alongside.

"Who's there?" said the sailor, quickly, in
alarm at such an unusual occurrence.

"Hush," said Ferris, springing upon the deck;
"we are officers of the law," then in a louder voice
he told the sailor to call Van Dusen up.

"Stand there at the head of the companion-
way," he said to his deputies, "and arrest any
one who tries to pass."

Then he went below himself, and waited near

the entrance of the little cabin for Van Dusen to appear.

"What is all this disturbance?" said Van Dusen, coming quickly into the cabin.

"I am here to arrest a man named Craik," said Mr. Ferris.

"Arrest Craik!" said Van Dusen, surprised and angry; "no, sir, Mr. Craik is my guest, and I will not allow him to be disturbed. Mr. Craik is an Englishman and under my protection. What is the charge against him?"

The unusual noise had by this time aroused the three guests of Van Dusen, who came quickly into the little cabin, Craik wholly dressed, and with a look of fierce determination upon his face.

"What is it, Van Dusen?" he said, as he came forward. "Did I not hear my name called?"

"Yes," said Ferris, stepping up to him; "I arrest you in the name of the law."

"Stand back," said Craik, fiercely, at the same time drawing and cocking a pistol, and retreating toward the companion-way, up which he then ran quickly.

"It is no use," said Ferris, coolly; "he will be stopped on deck by my men. He is a rascal, and although I am very sorry to disturb you and your guests, Mr. Van Dusen, he must go with me to-night."

Craik had hardly appeared upon the deck, when

he was seized on both sides by the two deputies; he shook them desperately off, however, and discharged his pistol, wounding one of the men in the arm; he then rushed quickly to the forward end of the deck, probably with the intention of jumping overboard, but here he was met by Mr. Campion, who, seizing him by the pistol arm, held him as in a vise. There was a short struggle, but Craik was no match for the giant strength of the lawyer, who soon threw him flat upon his back, where he firmly held him until assistance came.

"Put the bangles on him," said Ferris, who had now appeared upon the deck followed by the others; "he is a desperate villain."

Van Dusen was about to protest again when he saw Mr. Campion.

"Why, Mr. Campion, my dear sir, what does all this mean?" he said, excitedly.

"It means," said Mr. Campion, "that you and I have been harboring and associating with one of the blackest villains that ever breathed air foreign to a penitentiary. You have had a narrow escape, sir, from I know not what perfidy. This wretch, under the guise of friendship, was deliberately plotting to rob you, as he has frequently robbed others. He will be tried for burglaries in New Jersey and London, England, for forgery in Paris, for murder in Italy, and other offences too numerous to mention."

Here Craik, made desperate again by the lawyer's words, sprang toward him with uplifted hands, but was stopped by the deputy detectives; breaking away from them, however, he sprang toward the side of the yacht, evidently meaning to jump overboard, but Ferris dexterously tripped him up, and he was again secured.

Explanations followed, and Van Dusen gratefully thanked Campion, and apologized to Ferris, who then ordered Craik put into the boat. He was then taken away; all was quiet again, and after talking the matter over for awhile, Van Dusen and his guests retired for the night.

This adventure happening under the friendly cover of night, no one heard, no one saw, and no one knew of, except those who were directly interested; for when the bright purifying rays of the morning sun began to illuminate and glorify the scene of the disturbance and its beautiful surroundings, there was no visible evidence of the night's work, or that so foul a conspirator against morality and good living had been annihilated and swept away. .

He was gone, that was all ; nobody knew why. Van Dusen had enjoined strict secrecy from his men and his guests; and when the Van Twists and the people upon Cup Island inquired for Craik, the reply was that he had gone to New York and would probably not soon return. The injury which the sailor received upon his arm proved to be but a flesh wound, and not serious.

"I never took to that man Craik, or Crick, or whatever his name was," said Aunt Deb to her sister, when told that he had left Oldport. " He was allus a lickin' of a person all over, and a plasterin' on compliments, just as a snake will lick a bird afore he gobbles him down whole. Sich kind o' people is dangerous, an' I'm glad he likes New York company better'n he does ours. I shan't miss him a bit."

Thus Craik passed out of their little circle, and was not seriously missed by any member of it.

The day following his capture, Mr. Van Dusen sailed away on the " Siren" with his friends; and a few days later Nettie, accompanied by Mr. Campion, at her uncle's request, left for home; and it was not long after that the whole party, including the Van Twists, were on their way home; Tom and Jack to their respective duties in New York, cheered in mind and heart by bright and loving prospects for the future; Mrs. Tillottson, Belle, and Aunt Deborah to their home in Massachusetts, and the Van Twists to Florida, where they owned winter-quarters. The empty cottages were as usual left to the care of Sandy, and Cup Island once more resumed its appearance of peaceful seclusion.

CHAPTER XVI.

Ten Years elapse—Rome—Nettie at her Villa—Aunt Deborah writes from America—She contemplates Marriage—Bid's last Venture—Alice Van Twist a Widow—Matrimony in the Air.

THE passage of ten years brings many changes. Steps that were quick and vigorous become measured and deliberate; hair that was rich with the color of youth becomes gray and lifeless; loves that were ardent with the fires of youthful vitality are mellowed into a comfortable, satisfied routine of domestic felicity; cities rise up and decline, and nations gain ascendency and power, or lose prestige. So works that wizard Time.

It is March, and if the reader will accompany us to Rome, we will demonstrate how little ten years have accomplished in damaging the dispositions or appearance of our principal characters.

A little to the east of the Quirinal, and over by the church of S. Maria Maggiore, upon a beautifully shaded knoll near the road which connects with the Via Tiburtina, nestling among cypress-trees and shrubbery, is the villa which was formerly owned by Roger Dexter. Beautiful fountains send their spray into the warm Italian air, ornamenting picturesque lawns and flowery slopes.

24

The villa is alive with the joyous music of laughter and conversation.   It is the season of health, and our friends Dr. Tillottson and Nettie, his loving wife, with their three children, having spent the winter in England, are now, after an absence of four years, once more enjoying their beautiful Roman home.   They will make but a brief stay of perhaps three months, as they do not deem it safe to brave the malaria which comes after July, and has been, during the summer months, the curse of Rome for centuries.

Let us ascend the broad stone steps of this miniature palace before us, and as we do so, resting for a moment against the stately pillars of the portico, gaze back at the beautiful Italian landscape.

In the dim northern distance are the hazy outlines of the Sabine Mountains, towering Monte Gennaro and lower Montecelli; nearer we see the church Sant' Agnese, with charming cypress foliage and beautiful art-works in the foreground. We are indeed in Rome, the city of profound antiquity.   We walk reverentially to the other end of the portico to catch, if we can, a glimpse of St. Peter's dome, and as we hear from within the American clock strike the hour of four, we enter the house, crossing the handsomely-paved vestibule, and look into the dining-hall beyond.

The faces which meet us here are familiar.

Seated at the head of a long table is Tom Tillottson, stouter but little older looking than when we
last saw him upon Cup Island. Nettie, his wife,
sits opposite, and seems so youthful and fresh
that we can with difficulty realize the passage of
so much time. Mr. Campion sits by the side of
his good wife, whom we immediately recognize as
Tom's mother. They are a handsome elderly
couple, giving substantial proof to the theory that
matrimonial felicities smooth out the wrinkles of
time and bring health's bloom to the cheeks. By
her mother's side is Belle, now Mrs. Stratton, but
the chair next to her is vacant; it belongs to Jack.
On the opposite side of the table sit a few invited
guests, among whom we recognize Moses Wigand
and Professor Romney. At another table, near an
open window, which looks out upon the beautiful
scene we have just described, sit five rosy-cheeked,
healthy-looking children, in charge of a motherly-
looking nurse.

The conversation was animated and full of joyful exclamations, for the mail from America had
just arrived, and this was always a cause for great
rejoicing.

"Where is Jack?" said Mrs. Campion; "I want
him to hear me read Aunt Deborah's letter."

"I left him down at the Borghese gallery on the
Corso studying Cupids," said Belle, laughing. "He
will be here soon; he has found four pictures there

by Albani, called 'The Seasons,' which, I believe, have completely charmed his senses."

Just at this moment Jack entered; tall as ever, and with the same twinkle of fun radiating from the corners of his handsome eyes.

" These are the Cupids which have so completely charmed my senses," said Jack, with a loving look at his wife, and pointing at two of the five children at the other table.

As Jack took his seat with the rest, Mrs. Campion began to read Aunt Deb's letter:

" MY DEAR MARY,—Don't you think it's most time you folks was comin' home? I'm awfully lonesome here, an' it don't seem natural-like in this strange place. Seems to me two long years is a pretty good stretch for a weddin' trip. I go pokin' about the house a tellin' the girls what to do, and what not to do, an' try to pass away the time, but it drags dreadfully, an' it's no use, I'm lonesome.

" I s'pose Josie Campion is Josephine Evans by this time, judgin' from all you write an' what I hear. Well, I hope they'll be happy, an' never know what it is to want good bread an' sweet butter.

" There's something on my conscience to tell you, sister, but somehow it is pretty hard for me to get at it. Of course, you remember Mr. Sandy, or Samuel Sandy as his name is, and of course you remember how he lost his beloved wife some five years ago when we was there a summerin', an' was left a widower. Well, Mr. Sandy an' me has kind o' struck up a match. He was out here to see me, an' asked me to marry him, and it took more courage than I had to say no.

"He said he took to me immense after his wife died, an' he tho't I would make him a useful wife an' good companion. I allus liked Sam Sandy; there was nothin' lazy about him; he was allus smart as a whip. Well, to make a long story short, I told him I was a poor, good-for-nothin' old maid, and had the rumatiz fearful, but if he liked me, an' tho't I could make his life any happier, I'd have him.

"Sam wanted to have the knot tied right away, but I sent him home and told him I'd not get married anyway 'till you came back to Ameriky. So you see Mary, after all these years of pashent waitin' I am to get my reward. I hope he won't make me postmaster of Oldport, for I never was quick at readin' and writin', an', besides, I should be dyin' to read all the letters an' postal cards. I don't mind tendin' store, though, occasionally, for you can get to see folks that way without goin' to call on 'em.

"Tell Augustus that Sniffin, his head man, is engaged to marry Eleanor Bangs. Everybody is gettin' married, an' I' tho't it a good time to try it on myself.

"Sam said that the Van Twists were on Smoke Island last summer. The daughter, Mrs. Kendall, who married that preacher, you know, is a widder. Sam says that Mr. Kendall worked himself to death in New York, a lookin' after poor folks, startin' up missions and revivals, and such, an' that Mrs. Kendall was as crazy about it as he was. She has a little boy, an' Sam says he looks like the major. I s'pose it's all right for a preacher to do just as Mr. Kendall did, but for my part I never could chime in among them dirty folks we saw when we was in New York, an' talk natural-like to them. I should allus be thinkin' I was gettin' something on me, or a ketchin' some fever. Sam said the major looked old, an' I told Sam I tho't any man would look old if he was henpecked as that poor major was by that Van Twist woman. You see, I wanted Sam Sandy to destinctly understand that if I *was* an old maid there was no danger of his bein' henpecked an' hocus-pocussed as that poor old Major Van Twist was.

" Tell Augustus that I am tired of York State ; and as soon as you both get back I'm off for old Massachusetts, for I'm goin' to be married from the old home at W——.

" Sandy isn't a very stylish name, but it's better than Muddy, an' I'm goin' to try it anyhow. Deborah Tremane Sandy don't sound bad enough to skeer anybody. Come home as soon as you can, and give my love to all, babies and everybody.

"Your affectionate sister,

"DEBORAH TREMANE."

"Well, well," said Jack, after the amusement created by Aunt Deb's letter had somewhat subsided, "this will make Sandy our Uncle Sam. Quite appropriate for a postmaster; but how is it, Governor,"—Jack had always addressed Mr. Campion by that title, since he had married Mrs. Campion,—"how is it about Josephine and Bob Evans? I knew that Bob was awfully gone in that direction and thought a great deal of Josie, but I had no idea they would make a match of it."

Mr. Campion, who, like the others, had been looking over his mail, glanced up with a roguish smile and quietly remarked, "I always fancied Bob. He is a whole-souled, industrious sort of a Bohemian, and will make Jo a good husband; and I always gave her credit for taking care of herself; but it seems she, like all other frail women,"—a sly glance at Mrs. Campion,—"must have a protector. There's sister Deborah now; for years and years she has paddled her own canoe, and now at last she bows to the inevitable and links her fortunes with an Oldporter."

"I'm sure I don't know what to think of Deborah," said Mrs. Campion, looking strangely puzzled.

"As Aunt Deb says, there's matrimony in the air," said Tom, laughing; "there's Sniffin and Eleanor Bangs, too,—wonders never cease."

At this moment, when they were all full of that kindly feeling which is always begotten by the announcement of happy engagements, another old acquaintance quietly enters the room with an open letter in her hand; stepping up close to Mrs. Campion she says, in a whisper which is audible all over the room,—

"Shure ma'am, an' it's a hard duty oi have to tell ye. Oi must lave your sarvice intirely."

"Why, Bid," said Mrs. Campion, in great surprise at such a piece of news, "what *is* the matter?"

"Well, ma'am, ye see oi've jist been afther havin' a lether from me coozin in Oireland, an' shure it's him oi'm goin' to marry so long, an' now he writes that his poor father is dead an' lift him his property; an' Tim, that's his name, God bless him, says oi must come roight home, for he has divil a soul, poor man, to boil a potato for him, or look after his bedmakin' and the loikes o' that."

"Another county heard from," shouted Jack. "Bid, I congratulate you. May you live long and prosper, and may Mr. Tim's hearthstone never grow cold for the want of a stick, or a youngster to add it to the fire."

"Oh, la, Misther Jack," said Bid; "shure it's pate we burn in ould Oireland and not sticks, an' it's the loikes of you wid childer of your own would not begrudge a bairn or two to a poor old Oirish woman."

It was evident that Bid was happy as she retired amid the congratulations and good wishes which were showered upon her.

The people at the table were all happy, and, glad to see them thus, we quietly withdraw, trusting that Fate will deal gently with them in this foreign land.

THE END.

www.ingramcontent.com/pod-product-compliance
Lightning Source LLC
Chambersburg PA
CBHW020512270326
41926CB00008B/842